The Carpenter
A Model to Follow

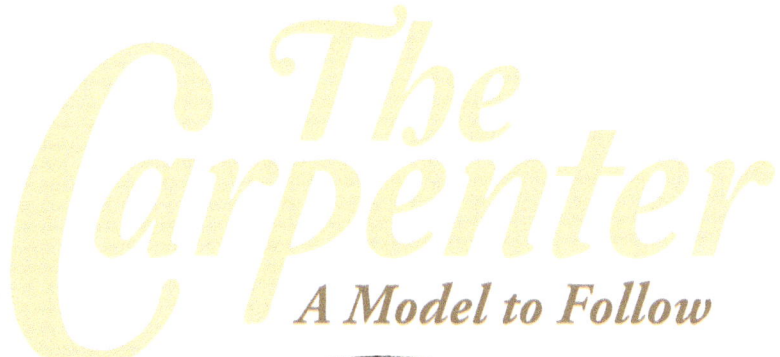

LEO PITTS

We find the title *carpenter* was given to Jesus by the local people with whom he was associated.

In Mark 6:3, they said, "Isn't this the carpenter, the son of Mary?"
(A further reference to this can be found in Matthew 13:55.)

Jesus lived with Mary and Joseph and his family for about thirty years, and it stands to reason that he would have been involved in supporting them alongside Joseph, who was a carpenter.

It was common practice for a father to pass on his skills to his sons.

WestBow Press books may be ordered through booksellers or by contacting:

WestBow Press
A Division of Thomas Nelson & Zondervan
1663 Liberty Drive
Bloomington, IN 47403
www.westbowpress.com
844-714-3454

Produced by Leo Pitts
Discovery Bay 3305
Victoria, Australia
Unless otherwise indicated, photos courtesy of The Lumo Project (Lumoproject.com).

Scriptures are taken from the World English Bible (WEB)
which is a Public Domain (no copyright) Modern English translation of the Holy Bible.

ISBN: 978-1-9736-9997-2 (sc)
978-1-9736-9998-9 (hc)
978-1-9736-9999-6 (e)

Library of Congress Control Number: 2023910965

Print information available on the last page.

WestBow Press rev. date: 06/30/2023

WESTBOW
PRESS®
A DIVISION OF THOMAS NELSON
& ZONDERVAN

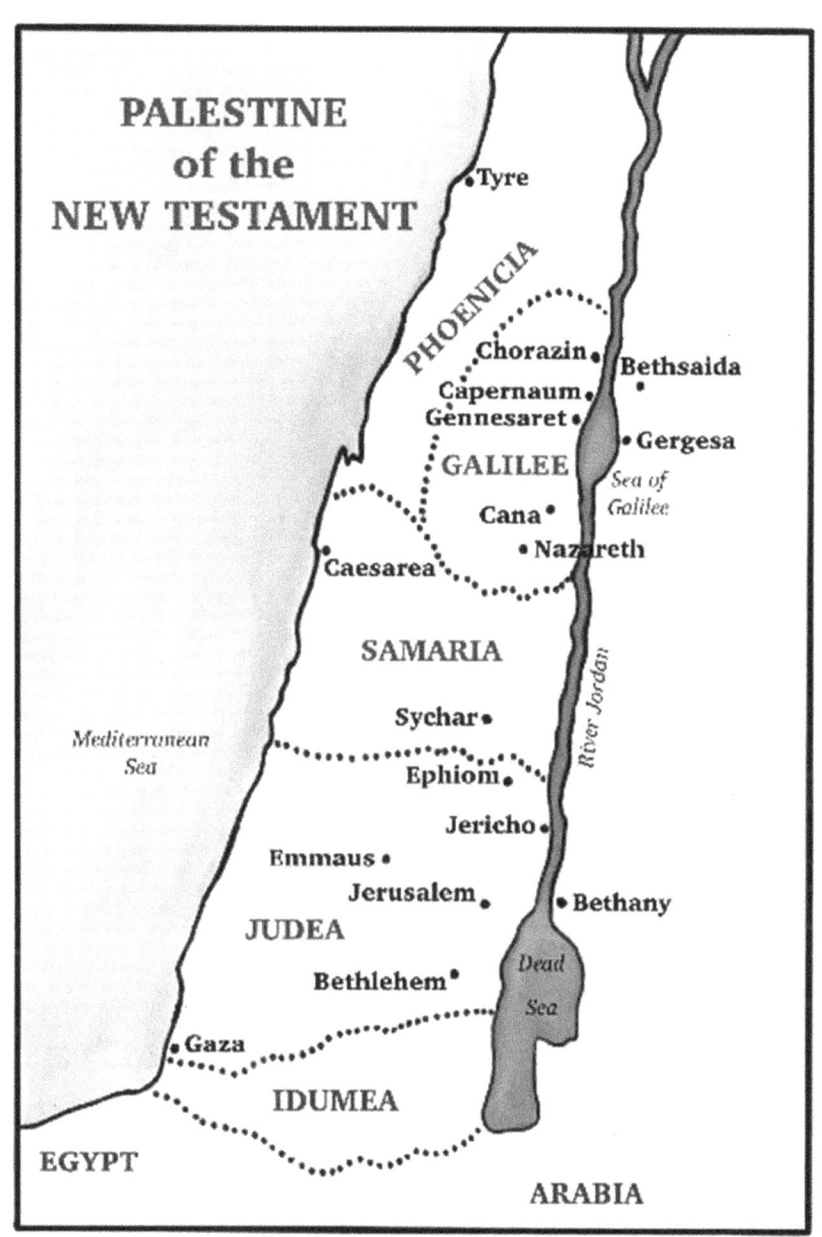

Map of Palestine in the New Testament

To Sophia

Readers may wonder why Sophia is mentioned here.
Sophia is the Greek word for *wisdom,*
and in Proverbs 8:22 she introduces herself in the line:
"Yahweh possessed me in the beginning of his work."

She is the integral essence of spirituality.

Without her, this book would not have been possible.

Acknowledgments

The author wishes to acknowledge and sincerely thank the World English Bible for their outstanding work, which has been used extensively in this book. WEB needs to be praised for not having copyright provisions. The Bible is for everyone! This sentiment is refreshingly found with those who kindly made available the many images at The Lumo Project.

All four evangelists—Matthew, Mark, Luke, and John—appear at various intervals throughout the text, but the sequences of their gospels have been altered to render the story of Jesus as a faithful representation of all four gospels into a single entity. This is really intended as an introduction to the gospels, with the hope that readers will more easily be able to grasp what the story of Jesus is about. All references to the texts have been included at the heading of each section so the reader will not be distracted with lots of cross-referencing. **It is important to understand here, that these references are merely guidelines and more often than not, extracts from longer passages have been used in order to keep the story flowing. Paraphrasing is used to a large extent and quotes are not necessarily verbatim as such.**

Paintings are from the Jan van 't Hoff collection, for which I am especially grateful.

I would like to thank my brother, Brian, for his amazingly detailed knowledge of scripture and especially for his years of research into the Messianic prophecies of Isaiah.

Finally, a big thanks to my daughter, Rachel, for her dedication and enthusiasm as an editor and strong supporter. She produced the map of Palestine in New Testament times.

CONTENTS

PREAMBLE

The nature of this text is designed specifically to tell the Gospel story to young people and others without the necessity of providing a vast amount of reference material, as this can be extremely daunting to initial readers. For those of you who wish to delve deeper into the story, it is suggested you consider expanding your horizons with one of the many volumes of the New Testament that are readily available. The New International Version (NIV) is quite modern and readable and is an alternate version to the World English Bible (WEB), which has been used extensively in this book.

Much of the material normally found in the New Testament—things like the genealogy of Jesus—have been purposefully omitted here in order to keep the story as vibrant as possible. These issues can be experienced with a study of a more complete version if one so wishes. Furthermore, much of the *theological* type of approach that is found in John's gospel has been modified into a more acceptable form. Similarly, the precision of the line-numbering system has been abandoned because all four of the original evangelists have been melded into a considered sequence, hopefully one that is more readily understood by novice readers. For example, one of the gospels mentions three talents, while another refers to ten talents—the evangelists were not unlike our present-day journalists writing for their own audiences, all trying to arrive at a particular perspective: in this case, the story of Jesus.

The significance of Jesus Christ was first mooted centuries before he appeared on Earth. Way back in the Babylonian/Assyrian days, one of the Jewish prophets—a dude known as Isaiah—predicted that these events would take place. By the way, the Babylonians were pretty smart. For example, they were the first to observe that the moon actually took nineteen years to complete a full cycle and go back to where it started.

Anyway, these invasions were happening during the eighth century BC, according to a considerable amount of cuneiform—a sunbaked clay tablet—information and ended up, to cut a long story short, with Assyria, its capital, Ashur on the Euphrates River in today's northwestern corner of Iraq, being the superior protagonist. In 734, Tiglath-Pileser III invaded Israel, instigating the Immanuel prophesy of Isaiah, about Yahweh saving Jerusalem. As a result, we are comfortable with our acceptance of the eventual appearance of Jesus coming to save us, his people.

INTRODUCTION

As young people, we all have so many dreams about life matters. It is absolutely normal to dream about all sorts of things, and some may be strange or weird and we don't know from where they come. From early days we come across anything from Donald Duck to Hairy McLary from Donaldson's Dairy, among a plethora of things we have had read to us and to which we are exposed on other media.

In other times and cultures, we experienced a myriad of concepts as to where we originated and where the "world" came from in such ancient Dreamtime stories of the Rainbow Serpent or that of Adam and Eve and so on. All these issues make their way into our subconscious and over time become an integral part of who we are. Our intellect processes a stunning array of inputs and includes others from the collective unconscious that was first mentioned by Carl Jung.

Without going into the intricacies of mental, psychological, and spiritual development, it is suffice to say that we all have extraordinary imaginations and use them as we journey through our personal approach to the meaning of life. From a Christian perspective, we learn from an early age that our souls are an extremely important element when considering the whole self, and we need to give them some attention in order to fully develop.

In early childhood we have our favorite doll or teddy bear and become quite attached to these inanimate toys—in a way we love them; we aren't discouraged from doing this as our parents know that such attachments are merely a precursor to more permanent things as we develop our relationships in life.

The concept of love is basic to the human condition, and we end up loving—after our mothers, our siblings, our pets, that new bike, and perhaps even a member of the opposite sex—oh no! When the object of our affection is not physically present, we substitute something—a photo, for example—and our love simply jumps into another realm. This might not be tangible, but it is nonetheless real. Without realizing it, we accept some sort of spiritual dimension to which we are totally aligned.

This story is about the love of God.

Dreams have a part to play here, and too often, we don't pay much attention to their content. When Martin Luther King Jr. announced his dream in the context of his magnificent attempt to draw attention to the plight of African Americans, the whole world sat up and paid attention. Dreams can be powerful tools for artists, scientists, inventors, and so on, and they often lead us to areas in our lives to which we might not otherwise venture.

The story of Jesus began with a dream by his mother, Mary.

1

Early Days

Beginnings: Luke 1:5–25

T he story of Jesus begins in the time when Herod the Great was king of Judea. There was a priest named Zechariah, who belonged to the priestly division of Abijah; his wife, Elizabeth, was a descendant of Aaron. They were both righteous before God, walking blamelessly in all the commands and ordinances of the Lord. They were childless because Elizabeth was unable to conceive, and they were both well advanced in years.

According to the custom of the priesthood, when Zechariah was on temple duty and was serving as priest before God, he was chosen to go into the temple sanctuary and burn incense. When the time came, all the worshippers were assembled outside, praying.

While Zechariah was inside, an angel of the Lord appeared to him, standing at the right side of the altar of incense.

When Zechariah saw him, he was troubled and became fearful.

But the angel said to him, "Don't be afraid, Zechariah, because your request has been heard, and your wife, Elizabeth, will bear you a son, and you shall call his name John. You will have joy and gladness, and many will rejoice at his birth, and he will be great in the sight of Yahweh. He will drink no wine nor other strong drink and even before he is born, he will be filled with the Holy Spirit. He will turn many of the children of Israel to the Lord their God, and in the spirit and power of Elijah, he will go before Yeshua and turn the hearts of fathers to their children and the disobedient to the wisdom of the just; he will make ready a people prepared for Yeshua."

Zechariah said to the angel, "How can I be sure of this? For I am an old man, and my wife is well advanced in years."

The angel answered him, "I am Gabriel, who stands in the presence of God, and I was sent to speak to you and to bring you this good news. Now, however, because you didn't believe my words, you will be silent and unable to speak until the day that these things happen in their proper time."

The people were waiting for Zechariah and wondered why he was taking so long. When he came out, he was unable to speak, and they perceived that he'd had a vision. He continued making signs to them and remained mute.

When his time of priestly service was over, he departed to his house.

After this, his wife, Elizabeth, became pregnant and hid herself for five months, saying, "Yahweh has done this for me in the days he has looked at me to take away my reproach among men."

Birth of Jesus Foretold: Luke 1:26–38

In the sixth month of Elizabeth's pregnancy, the same angel, Gabriel, was sent from God to Nazareth, a city in Galilee. He visited a virgin who was pledged to be married to a man named Joseph, of the house of David.

The virgin's name was Mary, and the angel said to her, "Rejoice, you highly favored one! The Lord is with you; blessed are you among women!"

But when she saw him, she was greatly troubled at the saying and considered what kind of salutation this might be. The angel said to her, "Don't be afraid, Mary, for you have found favor with God. You shall conceive and bring forth a son, and you shall call his name Yeshua. He will be great, and he will be called the Son of the Most High. The Lord God will give him the throne of his father, David, and he will reign over the house of Jacob forever, and there will be no end to his kingdom."

Mary said to the angel, "How can this be, seeing I am a virgin?"

The angel answered, "The Holy Spirit will come on you, and the power of the Most High will overshadow you. Therefore, also the holy one who is born from you will be called the Son of God. Behold, Elizabeth, your relative, also has conceived a son in her old age; and this is the the sixth month with her who was called barren. For everything spoken by God is possible."

"Behold the handmaid of the Lord," Mary answered. "Be it to me according to your word."

With that the angel left her.

Mary Visits Elizabeth: Luke 1:39–56

Mary arose in those days and went into the hill country with haste, into a city of Judea, and entered the house of Zechariah and greeted Elizabeth. When Elizabeth heard Mary's greeting, the baby leaped in her womb, and Elizabeth was filled with the Holy Spirit. She cried out in a loud voice and said, "Blessed are you among women, and blessed is the fruit of your womb! Why am I so favored, that the mother of my Lord should come to me? The moment the sound of your greeting reached my ears, the baby in my womb leaped for joy. Blessed is she who believed, for there will be a fulfillment of the things that have been spoken to her from the Lord!"

Mary said,

> "My soul magnifies the Lord,
> And my spirit rejoices in God my Savior,
> For he has looked upon
> The humble state of his handmaid.
> From now on all generations will call me blessed,
> For he who is mighty has done great things for me,
> And holy is his name.
> His mercy is for generations on generations.
> On those who fear him.
> He has shown strength with his arm.
> And has scattered the proud
> In the imagination of their hearts.
> He has put down princes from their thrones.
> But has exalted the lowly.
> He has filled the hungry with good things.
> But has sent the rich away empty-handed.
> He has helped his servant, Israel.
> And has remembered to be merciful,
> And he spoke to our fathers,
> To Abraham and his seed forever."

Mary visits Elizabeth
Courtesy of the lumoproject.com

Birth of John the Baptist: Luke 1:57–63

When it was time for Elizabeth to have her baby, she had a son. Her neighbors and relatives, upon hearing that the Lord had magnified his mercy to her, rejoiced with her. When they came to circumcise the child on the eighth day, they were going to name him after his father, Zechariah. His mother spoke up and said, "No, he is to be called John."

They pointed out to her, "None of your relatives is called by this name." So, they made signs to his father to find out what he wished the child's name to be. He signaled for a writing tablet, and to everyone's surprise, he wrote, "His name is John."

At that moment his mouth was opened, and his tongue loosed, and he began to speak, praising God.

The whole countryside marveled at these things and was abound with these happenings. All who heard the news asked, "What then will this child be? For the hand of the Lord was upon him."

Zechariah's Prophecy: Luke 1:67–80

Zechariah was filled with the Holy Spirit and said,

"Blessed be the Lord, the God of Israel, because he has visited and worked redemption for his people.
He has raised up a horn of salvation for us
In the house of his servant David,
As he spoke by the mouth of his holy prophets who have been from of old.
Salvation from our enemies
And from the hand of all who hate us.
To show mercy to our fathers
And to remember his holy covenant:
The oath he spoke to Abraham, our father,
To grant us that we, being delivered from the hand of our enemies,
Should serve him without fear,
In holiness and righteousness for all the days of our lives. You, my child, will be called a prophet of the Most High, for you will go before the face of the Lord to prepare his way.
To give the knowledge of salvation to his people

By the remission of their sins,
Because of the tender mercy of our God,
Who from on high will bring us the dawn light,
To shine on those living in darkness
And the shadow of death,
And to guide our feet into the way of peace."

The child grew up and became strong in spirit; he lived in the wilderness until he made his public appearance to Israel.

The Birth of Jesus: Luke 2:1–7

This was a time when Caesar Augustus issued a decree to take a census of the entire Roman population. Quirinus was governor of Syria at the time, and everyone was expected to enroll in their own city.

Joseph went up from Nazareth in Galilee to Bethlehem, the town of David, in Judea, because he belonged to the house and family of David. He went there with Mary, who was pledged to him as wife, being pregnant.

An angel of the Lord appeared to him in a dream and said, "Joseph, son of David, do not be afraid to take Mary home as your wife. The child she has conceived is by the power of the Holy Spirit. She will give birth to a son whom you are to name, Yeshua because he is the one who will save his people from their sins."

Joseph did not consummate their marriage until after the child was born.

While they were there, the time came for the baby to be born, and she gave birth to her firstborn, a son. She wrapped him in nursing clothes and placed him in an animal-feed basket because there were no rooms for them at the inn.

The Shepherds: Luke 2:8–20

In the fields nearby there were some shepherds keeping watch over their flocks at night. An angel of the Lord appeared to them, and they were terrified at the sight.

The angel said to them, "Do not be afraid. I bring you good news that will be a cause of great joy for all the people. Today in Bethlehem a Savior to you has been born; he is the Messiah! As a sign to you, you will find a baby wrapped in nursing clothes and lying in a manger."

At that, a multitude of angels appeared with the first angel and praised God, saying,

> "Glory to God in the highest heaven,
> And on earth peace, good will toward men."

When the angels left them, the shepherds said to each other, "Let's go to Bethlehem and see this thing that the Lord has told us about." They hurried off and found Mary and Joseph and the baby, who was lying in a feed trough. When they saw this, they spread the word about all they had been told about this child. All who heard it were amazed, and the shepherds returned, glorifying God.

Mary treasured all these things in her heart.

Circumcision of Jesus: Luke 2:21

On the eighth day it was time to circumcise the child. His name was called, Yeshua which had been told to Joseph in his dream and as Mary had been told by the angel Gabriel before Jesus was conceived in the womb.

Ancestry of Jesus: Matthew 1:1–17

The number of generations from Abraham to Jesus is three times fourteen: from Abraham to David there were fourteen; from David to the Babylonian deportation and exile there were fourteen; and fourteen from then to Jesus.

Visit of the Wise Men: Matthew 2:1–12

After the birth of Jesus in Bethlehem, during the time of King Herod, some wise men from the east came to Jerusalem and asked, "Where is the newborn king of the Jews? We saw his star as it rose and have come to pay homage."

When Herod heard this, he became greatly disturbed, along with all the people in Jerusalem. He called together all the chief priests and teachers of the law and asked them where the Messiah was to be born.

"In Bethlehem of Judea," they informed him, "for this is what the prophet has written:
'You Bethlehem in the land of Judah
Are by no means least among the princes of Judah.
For out of you will come a ruler
Who will shepherd my people, Israel.'"

Then Herod secretly called the wise men to him and found from them the exact time of the star's appearance. He sent them to Bethlehem after having instructed them, "Go and search diligently for the child, and after you have found him, bring me word so that I also may come and worship him."

After they heard this from Herod, they went on their way. The star they had seen in the east went ahead of them until it stood over the place where the child was. Being astrologers, they were overjoyed at seeing the star. When they went into the house, they saw the child with his mother, Mary. They bowed down, worshipped him, opened their treasures, and offered him gifts of gold, frankincense, and myrrh.

After they received a message in a dream not to go back to Herod, they returned to their own country another way.

Presentation in the Temple: Luke 2:22–35

When the time came for the purification rites required by the law of Moses, Joseph and Mary took Jesus to Jerusalem to present him to the Lord, as it written in the law that: *every firstborn male is to be consecrated to the Lord*. In keeping with what was said, *a pair of doves or two young pigeons were to be sacrificed.*

Now there was a man in Jerusalem called Simeon, who was righteous and devout and awaited the consolation of Israel, and the Holy Spirit was upon him. It had been revealed to him that he would not experience death before he had seen the Anointed One of the Lord. Inspired by the Spirit, he went into the temple courts. When the parents brought in the child Jesus to perform for him the customary ritual of the law, Simeon took Jesus in his arms and praised God, saying:

"Now Almighty God, you can release your servant in peace,
As you have fulfilled your promise to me.
My eyes have seen your salvation.
Which you have prepared before the face of all peoples.
A light for revelation to the nations
And the glory of your people, Israel."

The child's father and mother marveled at what was said about him. Simeon then blessed them and said to Mary: "This child is destined to cause the downfall and the rising of many in Israel and to be a sign that will be spoken against. The thoughts of many hearts will be revealed, and a sword will pierce your own soul."

The Prophetess: Luke 2:36–39

There was also a prophetess, Anna, who was the daughter of Penuel, of the tribe of Asher. She was very old, having lived with her husband during their seven years of marriage after which she was widowed; she was eighty-four years old. She never left the temple and worshipped there day and night, fasting and praying. At that very moment she came up to them and gave thanks to God and told everyone about this child and how they could look forward to the redemption of Israel.

The Flight into Egypt: Matthew 2:13–15

An angel suddenly appeared to Joseph in a dream, saying: "Arise and take the child and his mother and flee to Egypt and stay there until I tell you, for Herod will seek the young child to destroy him." Joseph got up and that very night took the child and his mother to Egypt. They stayed there until Herod died and was replaced by his son. This fulfilled the prophecy: "Out of Egypt I have called my son."

The Innocents: Matthew 2:16–18

In the meantime, when Herod saw that he had been mocked by the wise men, he was exceedingly angry and sent out and killed all the male children in and around Bethlehem from two years old and under, according to the exact time he had learned from the wise men.

What was said through Jeremiah, the prophet, was fulfilled:

"A voice was heard in Ramah.
Lamentation, weeping and great mourning.
Rachel weeping for her children,
She wouldn't be comforted because they are no more."

Return to Nazareth: Matthew 2:19–24

When Herod was dead, the angel appeared to Joseph in Egypt in a dream and said, "Arise and take the child and his mother and go into the land of Israel, for those who sought the young child's life are now dead."

Joseph took the child and his mother into the land of Israel. He heard that Archelaus was reigning over Judea in the place of his father, Herod, so he went to a region in Galilee. There he settled in a town called Nazareth, which was why it was said that he would be called a Nazarene.

The child grew to maturity, and he was filled with wisdom.

The Boy Jesus in the Temple: Luke 2:41–52

Every year, Jesus's parents went to Jerusalem for the festival of the Passover. On one of these occasions, when Jesus was twelve, they went as usual for the celebration. After it was over, they made their way home but unknown to them, Jesus stayed on in Jerusalem. Thinking he was with the others in the party, they travelled without him for a day. When they looked for him among their relatives and friends, they could not find him. They returned to Jerusalem and searched for him for three days and eventually found him sitting in the temple courts among the teachers, listening to them and asking questions. Everyone who heard him was amazed at his understanding and his answers.

When his parents saw him, they were relieved as well as astonished.

His mother said, "Son, why have you done this to us? Your father and I have been searching for you anxiously."

Jesus answered, "Why were you searching for me? Did you not know that I had to be in my Father's house?"

But they failed to understand what he was saying.

Then he went down to Nazareth with them and was obedient. His mother treasured in her heart all these things, and Jesus, for his part, progressed steadily in wisdom and grace and increased in favor with God and men.

Prelude to Public Ministry: Luke 3:1–2

In the fifteenth year of the rule of Tiberius Caesar, when Pontius Pilate was procurator of Judea, when Herod was tetrarch of Galilee and his brother, Phillip, tetrarch of the region Ituraea and Trachonitis, while Lysanias was tetrarch of Abilene, in the high priesthood of Annas and Caiaphas, the word of God came to John, the son of Zechariah, while he was out in the wilderness.

John the Baptist: Luke 3:3–18

He went about the entire region around the Jordan, proclaiming a baptism of repentance for the forgiveness of sins. As is written in Isaiah:

> "A voice of one calling in the wilderness,
> Prepare the way for the Lord.
> Make straight paths for him.
> Every valley shall be filled.
> Every mountain and hill levelled.
> The winding roads shall be made straight,
> And the rough way smoothed.
> All humanity shall see the salvation of God."

John said to the crowds coming to be baptized by him, *you brood of vipers, who warned you to flee from the coming wrath? Produce some evidence in keeping with repentance. Don't begin by telling yourselves that Abraham is your father, for I tell you that God can raise up children for Abraham out of these very stones. The axe is already at the root of every tree and every tree that does not produce good fruit will be cut down and thrown on the fire.*

The crowd asked: "What shall we do then?"

John replied: "Anyone who has two shirts should give one to the person who has none, and anyone who has food should share it with those who haven't any."

Tax collectors who came to him to be baptized asked: "Teacher, what should we do?"

He answered: "Exact nothing over and above that which is required of you."

Soldiers likewise asked him: "And what should we do?"

He answered: "Don't accuse people falsely or bully them; and be content with your pay."

The people were full of anticipation and wondered in their hearts if he might possibly be the Messiah. John became aware of this and said to them, "I am baptizing you with water, but there is one to come who is much more powerful than I, and I am not worthy to loosen the straps on his sandals.

"He will baptize you with fire and the Holy Spirit; his winnowing fork is in his hand, and he will clear his threshing floor and gather the grain into his barn while he will burn the chaff in an unquenchable fire."

With powerful exhortations of this nature, he proclaimed the good news to the people.

Baptism of Jesus: Luke 3:21–22

When all the people were being baptized, Jesus came down from Nazareth in Galilee and was baptized in the Jordan by John. No sooner had he come up out of the river than John saw the heavens open, and the Holy Spirit descended on Jesus like a dove and a voice came from heaven, saying: "You are my beloved Son. In you I am well pleased."

Temptations of Jesus: Luke 4:1–13

Jesus, full of the Holy Spirit, left the Jordan and was led by the Spirit into the desert for forty days, being tempted by the devil. He ate nothing during that time and at the end of it was hungry.

The devil said to him, "If you are the Son of God, tell these stones to turn into bread."

Jesus answered, "It is written, 'Man shall not live by bread alone but by every word that proceeds out of the mouth of God.'"

Then the devil took him up an exceedingly high mountain and showed him all the kingdoms of the world in an instant. He said to Jesus, "The power and glory of all these kingdoms has been given to me; if you worship me in homage, it will all be yours."

Jesus said, "It is written, 'You shall worship the Lord your God and you shall serve him only.'"

Then the devil led him to Jerusalem and had him stand on the pinnacle of the temple and said to him, "If you are the Son of God, throw yourself down from here, for it is written: 'He will put his angels in charge of you. On their hands they will bear you up so that you don't dash your foot against a stone."

Jesus answered: "Again, it is written, 'You shall not test the Lord, your God.'"

Then the devil left him, and the angels came and served him.

2

Mission Beginnings

The Ministry Begins: John 1:29–39;

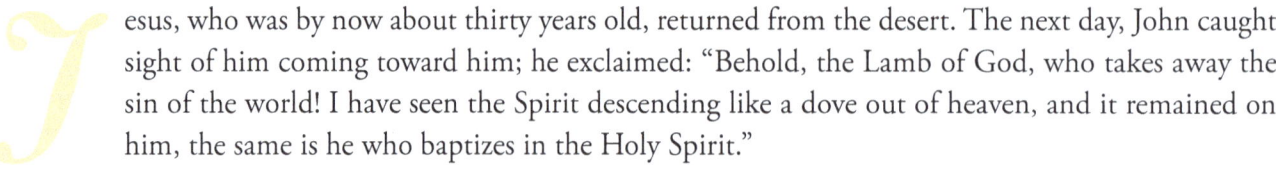

esus, who was by now about thirty years old, returned from the desert. The next day, John caught sight of him coming toward him; he exclaimed: "Behold, the Lamb of God, who takes away the sin of the world! I have seen the Spirit descending like a dove out of heaven, and it remained on him, the same is he who baptizes in the Holy Spirit."

Two of John's disciples heard what he said and went to follow Jesus.

When Jesus turned around and noticed them following, he asked, "What are you looking for?"

They said to him, "Rabbi, where do you stay?"

Jesus answered, "Come and see."

The First Disciples: John 1:39–42; Matthew 4:18–22; Luke 5:1–11

So they went to see where he was lodged and stayed with him that day. One of the two who stayed with him was Simon Peter's brother Andrew.

The next day they went down to the lake at Gennesaret, and the first thing Andrew did was go to his brother Simon, who was a fisherman.

He brought him to Jesus, who looked at him and said, "You are Simon, son of John; from now on you shall be called Cephas" (Peter).

People were crowding around him and listening to him talking about God. The crowd was so overwhelming that Jesus got into Simon's boat and asked him to pull away from the shore, and he taught the people from the boat.

When he had finished speaking to the crowd, he said to Simon, "Pull out into the deep and let down your nets for a catch."

Simon answered, "Master, we've worked hard all night and haven't caught a thing; but because you say so I will let down the nets."

When they did this, they caught such an enormous number of fish that their nets were almost breaking, and they signaled to their mates in the other boat to come give them a hand. Both boats were filled to the point of sinking. When Simon Peter saw this, he and his partners—the Zebedee boys—were totally astonished.

Simon fell at Jesus's knees and said, "Go away from me, Lord, I am a sinful man."

Jesus said to him: "Come after me and I will make you fishers for men."

Jesus calls his disciples
Courtesy of the lumoproject.com

The Wedding at Cana: John 2:1–11

There was a wedding at Cana in Galilee, and Jesus and his disciples had been invited; Jesus's mother was also there. After a while, the wine was about to run out, and Jesus's mother said to him, "They have no more wine."

Jesus replied, "Woman, what does that have to do with you and me? My hour has not yet come."

His mother said to the servants, "Do whatever he tells you."

Nearby there were six stone ceremonial water jars, each with a capacity of about twenty to thirty gallons.

Jesus said to the servants, "Fill the water pots with water."

They filled them to the brim.

Then he told them, "Now draw some off and take it to the ruler of the feast."

They did so, and the ruler of the feast tasted the water that had been turned into wine. He didn't know where it had come from.

He went to the bridegroom and called him aside and said, "Everyone serves the good wine first and then bring out then, when the guests have drunk freely, that which is worse, but you have saved the best until now."

Jesus performed this, the first of his miracles in Cana of Galilee. Thus, did he reveal his glory, and his disciples believed in him.

The wedding at Cana
Courtesy of the lumoproject.com

Galilee: Mark 1:21–45

He then went down to Capernaum, and on the Sabbath, he taught the people. They were amazed at his teaching because he did it with authority.

In the synagogue was a man possessed by an impure spirit who shrieked in a loud voice, "Leave us alone, Jesus of Nazareth. Have you come to destroy us? I know who you are: the Holy One of God."

Jesus said sternly, "Be quiet! Come out of him."

Then the demon threw the man down before them and came out without injuring him. All the people were amazed and said to each other, "What words these are. With authority, he commands even the unclean spirits, and they obey him."

His renown kept spreading throughout the countryside.

Jesus left the synagogue and went to the house of Simon. Simon's mother-in-law was suffering from a high fever, and they asked Jesus to help her. So, he took her by the hand and raised her up. The fever left her, and she got up and served them.

At sunset, the people brought to Jesus those with all sorts of illnesses. Laying his hands on each of them, he healed them all; demons came out of many of them, shouting, "You are the Son of God." He preferred that the demons remained quiet, because they knew he was the Messiah.

At daybreak, Jesus went out to a solitary place. The people went looking for him and tried to stop him from leaving.

But he said to them, "I must proclaim the good news of the kingdom of God to other towns too, because that is why I was sent." And he continued preaching in the synagogues of Judea.

When he was in one of the towns, a man covered in leprosy came to him and fell on the ground in front of him, saying, "Lord, if you want to, you can make me clean."

Jesus reached out his hand and touched the man, saying, "I want to. Be clean!"

Immediately the leprosy left him.

Jesus ordered him, "See you say nothing to anybody, but go, show yourself to the priests and offer the things that Moses commanded for your cleansing as a testimony to them."

Yet the news about him spread so that the crowds came to him from everywhere.

Rejected in Nazareth: Luke 4:16–30

He came to Nazareth where he had been brought up and entered the synagogue on the Sabbath, as was his custom. He stood up to read, and the scroll of the prophet Isaiah was handed to him.

He unrolled it at the place where it was written:

> "The spirit of the Lord is upon me,
> Because he has anointed me to preach good news to the poor.
> To proclaim release to the captives, recovering of sight to the blind,
> To deliver those who are crushed,
> And to proclaim the acceptable year of the Lord."

Then he rolled up the scroll, gave it back to the attendant, and sat down. Everyone in the synagogue fixed their eyes on him.

He said to them, "Today this scripture has been fulfilled in your hearing."

All who heard him wondered at the gracious words which proceeded out of his mouth. "Isn't this Joseph's son?" they said.

Jesus said to them, "You will doubtless quote me this parable: 'Physician, heal yourself!' Whatever we have heard done in Capernaum, do also here in your hometown.

"Most certainly I tell you, no prophet is acceptable in his hometown. Let me remind you that there were many widows in Israel in Elijah's time when the sky was shut for three and a half years and there a great famine came over the land. It wasn't to any of these that Elijah was sent, but to a widow in Zarephath in the region of Sidon. And there were many lepers in Israel at that time, yet the only one cleansed was Naaman, the Syrian."

All the people were filled with wrath when they heard this. They got up, drove Jesus out of town, and took him to the brow of the hill on which the town was built so that they might throw him off the cliff. But he just simply walked right through the throng and went on his way.

A Paralytic Forgiven and Healed: Mark 2:1–12

One day Jesus was teaching. Pharisees and teachers of the law from all over the countryside were there. The power of the Lord was with Jesus to heal the sick, and some men carried a paralyzed man on a mat; they tried to take him into the house, but because of the crowd were unable. So they went up on the roof and lowered him on his mat down through the tiles into the middle of the crowd, right in front of Jesus.

When Jesus saw their faith, he said, "Son, your sins are forgiven you."

The Pharisees and teachers of the law began thinking and muttering among themselves. "Who is this fellow who speaks blasphemy? God is the only one who can forgive sins."

Jesus perceived what they were saying and asked, "Why do you reason these things in your hearts? What is easier to say to the paralyzed man: 'Your sins are forgiven,' or 'Get up and walk'? But I want you to know that the Son of Man has authority on earth to forgive sins."

So, he said to the paralyzed man, "I say to you, get up, take up your mat, and go to your house."

Immediately he stood in front of them, picked up his mat, and went home praising God. All those present were amazed and gave praise to God, saying, "We have never seen anything like this before."

The Call of Levi: Mark 2:13–17

After this, Jesus was walking along the shore of the lake, and he spotted a tax collector named Levi, sitting in his booth.

"Follow me," Jesus said to him, and Levi got up, left everything, and followed him.

Levi then held a banquet for Jesus at his house, and a large crowd of tax collectors and others were there. The Pharisees and teachers of the law had their own special group and said to Jesus's disciples, "Why do you eat and drink with tax collectors and sinners?"

Jesus heard this and answered them: "Those who are healthy have no need for a physician, but those who are sick. I have not come to call the righteous, but sinners to repentance."

Questions about Fasting: Mark 2:18–22

They said to him, "John's disciples often fast and pray, and so do the disciples of the Pharisees, but yours go on eating and drinking."

Jesus answered, "Can you make the friends of the bridegroom fast while he is with them? But the time will come when the bridegroom will be taken from them; then they will fast."

He told them this parable: "No one takes a piece of unshrunken cloth to patch an old garment; if he does, the patch pulls away and the tear gets worse. Similarly, no one pours new wine into old wineskins; the new wine will burst them; the wine will run out and the wineskins destroyed."

Jesus Is Lord of the Sabbath: Mark 2:23–28; Luke 6:1–5

One Sabbath, Jesus was walking through the grain fields and his disciples began picking ears of grain, rubbing them through their hands and eating the kernels.

Some Pharisees asked, "Why are you doing what is unlawful on the Sabbath?"

Jesus answered them: "Have you never read what David did when he and those who were with him were hungry? He entered the house of God and took the bread, which was consecrated and which only the priests were permitted to have and shared it with those who were with him."

Then Jesus said to them, "The Sabbath was made for man, not man for the Sabbath. The Son of Man is lord of the Sabbath."

On another Sabbath, he went into the synagogue and was teaching, and a man was there whose right hand was withered. The Pharisees and teachers of the law were there and were watching him closely to see if they could find a reason to accuse him of healing on the Sabbath.

Jesus knew what they were thinking and said to the man, "Get up and stand in front of everyone."

The man got up and stood there.

Jesus said to them, "Is it lawful on the Sabbath to do good or to do harm, to save a life or kill?"

He looked around at them and then said to the man, "Stretch out your hand."

He did so, and his hand was completely restored. The Pharisees and teachers of the law were furious and began a discussion as to what they could do about Jesus.

The Twelve Apostles Chosen: Mark 3:13–19

Then he went out on to the mountainside to pray and spent the night conversing with God. At daybreak he called his disciples and selected twelve of them to be his apostles: Simon, to whom he gave the name Peter, his brother Andrew; the sons of Zebedee—James and John—to whom he gave the name Boanerges, meaning Sons of Thunder; Phillip; Bartholomew; Thomas; and Matthew—known as Levi, the tax collector; James, son of Alphaeus; Thaddaeus; Simon of the Zealot party; and Judas Iscariot, who also betrayed him.

Mission of the Twelve: Matthew 10:1–42

He addressed the twelve apostles to send them out on a mission. He gave them authority to expel unclean spirits and to heal every disease and sickness.

He said, "Go after the lost sheep of Israel and as you go, announce 'The kingdom of heaven is at hand' Provide yourselves with no gold or silver in your money belts as you will be provided with what you need; after all every laborer is worth his food. Into whatever city or village, you enter, find out who in it is worthy and stay there until you go on. He who welcomes you welcomes me, and who welcomes me welcomes him who sent me. And I tell you, whoever gives a cup of cold water to one who is a disciple of mine will not want for his reward."

When Jesus had finished instructing the twelve, he left that locality to preach and teach in other towns.

The Sermon on the Mount: Luke 6:17–26

His disciples, along with a great number of people from all over Judea, from Jerusalem and from the coastal regions around Tyre and Sidon, had come to hear him and be healed of all sorts of diseases, as well as those who were troubled by unclean spirits. On seeing such a large crowd, he went out on to the mountain with them and came to a level place. Those with impure spirits were cured, and they all tried to touch him because power came out from him and healed them all.

Looking at the disciples, he said,

Blessed are you, who are poor,
For yours is the kingdom of God.
Blessed are you who hunger now,
For you will be filled.
Blessed are you who weep now,
For you will laugh.
Blessed are you when men hate you,
When they exclude and mock you
And reject your name as evil,
For the sake of the Son of Man.
Rejoice in that day and leap for joy,
For great is your reward in heaven.
For their fathers did the same thing to the prophets.
But woe to you who are rich! For you have already received your reward.
Woe to you who are full now, for you will go hungry.
Woe to you who laugh now, for you will mourn and weep,
Woe when men speak well of you, for their fathers did the same thing to the false prophets."

Jesus Addresses All Who Are Listening: Luke 6:27–36

"Love your enemies, do good to those who hate you; bless those who curse you and pray for those who mistreat you. When someone strikes you on the cheek, offer also the other one; if someone takes your cloak, give him your coat as well. Give to all who ask and if anyone takes what belongs to you, do not ask for it back.

"Do to others as you would have them do to you. If you only love those who love you, what credit is in that for you? Even sinners love those who love them. Similarly, if you do good to those who do good to you, where is the credit in that? If you only lend to those from whom you expect repayment, there is no credit in that either. Love your enemies, do good to them, lend without expecting repayment. Your reward will be great, and you will be called children of the Most High, because he is kind to the ungrateful and wicked. Be merciful just as your Father is merciful."

Judging Others: Luke 6:37–45

"Do not judge and you will not be judged. Do not condemn and you will not be condemned. Set free and you will be set free. Give, and it will be given to you: a full measure, pressed down, shaken, and running over will be poured into your lap. For the measure you use will be the one you receive back."

He spoke a parable to them. "Can the blind lead the blind? Won't they both fall into the pit? The student is not above the teacher, but everyone who is fully trained will be like his teacher. Why do you look at the speck of sawdust in your brother's eye and fail to see the beam that is in your own eye? You hypocrite, first take the beam out of your own eye and then you will see clearly to remove the speck from your brother's eye. No good tree bears bad fruit, nor does a bad tree bear good fruit. Each tree is recognized by its own fruit. Figs aren't picked from thorns or grapes from a bramble bush. A good man brings good things out of the good stored up in his heart, and an evil man brings out evil things from the evil stored in his. For the mouth speaks what the heart is full of."

The Wise and Foolish Builders: Luke 6:46–49

"Why do you call me, 'Lord, Lord,' and do not do what I say? Everyone who comes to me hears my words and does them, is like a man building a house who digs down deep and lays the foundation on rock. When the flood came, the stream broke against that house but could not shake it. But the one who hears my words and does not do them is like a man who builds a house on the ground without a foundation. The moment that house was struck by the stream, it fell, and the ruin of that house was great."

3

Man of Many Miracles

The Faith of the Centurion

Jesus Raises a Widow's Son

Jesus Hears about John the Baptist

The Impertinent Towns

Jesus Anointed by a Sinful Woman

Jesus and Beelzebub

The Sign of Jonah

Pharisees and Experts in the Law

The Faith of the Centurion: Matthew 8:5–13

s Jesus entered Capernaum, a centurion whose servant was sick and about to die heard that Jesus was in town and came to him, saying, "Lord, my servant lies in the house, paralyzed and grievously tormented."

Jesus said to him, "I will come and heal him."

The centurion answered, "Lord, I'm not worthy for you to come under my roof. Just say the word and my servant will be healed. For I also am a man under authority with soldiers under me; I tell this one, 'Go,' and he goes; and to this one, 'Come,' and he comes; I say to my servant, 'Do this,' and he does it."

When Jesus heard this, he was amazed at him. Turning to the crowd following him, he said, "I tell you, I have not found such great faith, even in Israel. Go let it be done for you, as you have believed."

Jesus Raises a Widow's Son: Luke 7:11–17

Soon afterward, Jesus went to a town called Nain, and some disciples and a large crowd went along with him. As he approached the town gate, a dead person was being carried out—the only son of his mother, who was a widow. A large crowd was with her, and when Jesus saw her, his heart went out to her, and he said, "Don't cry."

Then he went up and touched the bier on which the boy lay, while the bearers stood still. He said, "Young man, I say to you, get up!"

The young man sat up and began to talk, and Jesus gave him back to his mother. They were all filled with awe and praised God, saying, "A great prophet has arisen among us; God has visited his people."

This news about Jesus spread throughout Judea and the surrounding region.

Jesus Hears of John the Baptist: Luke 7:18–35

By now, Herod had put John in prison because of his opposition to him taking his brother's wife. While he was there, his disciples were telling him all about the things Jesus was doing, so John sent them to ask him, "Are you the one who is to come, or should we expect someone else?"

Jesus replied, "Go back and tell John what you have seen and heard: the blind receive their sight, the lame walk, lepers are cleansed, the deaf hear, and the dead are raised up. The good news is preached to the poor; blessed is he who is not offended because of me."

When John's messengers set off, Jesus spoke to the crowd about John: "What did you go out into the wilderness to see? A reed shaken in the wind? A man dressed in fine clothes? Those who wear such clothes and live delicately are in palaces. So, what did you see? A prophet? Yes, indeed; this is he of whom it is written: 'I will send my messenger ahead of you to prepare your way before you.'

"I tell you that of all those born of a woman, there is not a greater prophet than John, and yet the one who is the least born into the kingdom of God is even greater than he. Heed carefully what you are hearing! What comparison can I use to describe this generation? They are like children sitting in the town square, calling to each other: 'We played the pipes for you, and you did not dance. We mourned for you, and you didn't cry.'

"For John came neither eating bread nor drinking wine, and you said: 'He has a demon.' The Son of Man comes eating and drinking, and you say, 'He is a glutton and a drunkard and a friend of tax collectors and sinners.' Wisdom is justified by all her children."

The Impenitent Towns: Luke 10:10–15

Jesus began to reproach the towns where he had performed many of his miracles and they had failed to reform: "It will not go well with you, Chorazin! Woe to you, Bethsaida! If the miracles worked in you had taken place in Tyre and Sidon, they would have repented long ago sitting in sackcloth and ashes. On the day of judgment, it will be more tolerable for them. As for you, Capernaum, who are exalted to the heavens, you will be brought down to hades."

Jesus Anointed by a Sinful Woman: Luke 7:36–50

One of the Pharisees invited Jesus to have dinner at his house. A local woman who was a sinner heard that Jesus was eating at the Pharisee's house, so she came there with an alabaster jar of ointment. While Jesus was reclining at the table, she went behind him, weeping at his feet and wet his feet with her tears. Then she wiped them with her hair, kissed them, and anointed them with ointment.

A "sinful woman" washes Jesus' feet
Courtesy of the lumoproject.com

When the Pharisee who had invited him saw this, he said to himself, *If this man were a prophet, he would know what kind of woman this is who is touching him, that she is a sinner.*

Jesus said to him, "Simon, I have something to say to you."

"Tell me, teacher," he said.

"Two people owed money to a money lender; one owed him five hundred denarii and the other fifty. Neither of them had the money to pay him back, so he forgave the debts. Who of them therefore will love him most?"

Simon replied, "I suppose the one who had the bigger debt forgiven."

Jesus said, "You have judged correctly."

Then he turned to the woman and said to Simon, "Do you see this woman? I came into your house; you did not give me any water for my feet, but she has wet my feet with her tears and wiped them with her hair. You did not greet me with a kiss, but she has not stopped kissing my feet. You did not pour oil on my head, but she has anointed my feet with ointment. Therefore, I tell you, her many sins have been forgiven, as she has shown great love. But whoever has been forgiven little loves little."

Then Jesus said to her, "Your sins are forgiven."

The other guests began to say among themselves, "Who is this that forgives sins?"

Jesus said to the woman, "Your faith has saved you; go in peace."

Jesus and Beelzebub: Luke 11:14–28

A possessed man, who was deaf and mute, was brought to Jesus and he drove the demon out and cured the man. The crowd was amazed, but some said, "He drives out demons by Beelzebub, the prince of demons." Others tested him by asking for a sign from heaven.

Jesus knew their thoughts and said to them, "Any kingdom divided against itself will be brought to desolation, and a house divided against itself will fall. If Satan is divided against himself, how can his kingdom stand? I say this because you say that I drive out demons by Beelzebub. If I do, by whom do your followers drive them out? So, then they will be your judges. But if I drive out demons by the finger of God, then the kingdom of God has come to you. When a strong man, fully armed, guards his own house, his goods are safe. But when someone stronger attacks and overpowers him, he takes away the armor in which the man trusted and divides up his spoils.

"Whoever is not with me is against me and who does not gather with me scatters. When an impure spirit comes out of a person, it goes through arid places seeking rest but does not find any. Then it says, 'I will return to the house I left.' When it arrives, it finds the house swept clean and put in order. Then it finds seven other spirits more wicked than itself, and they all go and live there; the last state of that man is worse than the first.

"Every sin and every blasphemy can be forgiven, but blasphemy against the Holy Spirit will never be forgiven. Whoever says something against the Son of Man can be forgiven, but anything against the Holy Spirit will never be forgiven in this age or in the age to come."

As Jesus was saying these things, a woman in the crowd called out, "Blessed is the mother who gave you birth and nursed you.'

He replied, "Blessed rather are those who hear the word of God and keep it."

The Sign of Jonah: Luke 11:29–36

Some of the Pharisees and teachers of the law then spoke up, saying, "Teacher, we want to see you work some sign."

Jesus was annoyed at being asked for a sign and reminded them how Jonah had been a sign to the Ninevites, and the how the Queen of the South had come from the ends of the earth to hear the wisdom of Solomon.

He indicated to them that the only sign would be just like the sign of Jonah who was in the whale's belly for three days, so also would the Son of Man be in the belly of the earth for three days.

Then Jesus said, "Behold, one greater than Solomon is here, and one greater than Jonah is here."

"No one lights a lamp and puts it in a cellar or under a basket but on a stand that those who come in may see the light. Your eye is the lamp of your body; when your eyes are healthy, your whole body is full of light. When they are unhealthy, your body is full of darkness. See that the light within you isn't darkness and then the whole of your body will be full of light."

Pharisees and Experts in the Law: Luke 11:37–53

When Jesus finished speaking, a Pharisee invited him to eat with him. He went in and sat at the table. The Pharisee was surprised when he noticed that Jesus did not wash before the meal.

Jesus said to him, "You Pharisees clean the outside of the cup and dish, but inside you are full of greed and wickedness. You foolish people! Did not the one who made the outside, make the inside too? But give what is within you for gifts to the needy and everything will be made clean for you. Woe to you Pharisees, because you give God one tenth of all your mint, rue and all kinds of garden herbs, but you bypass justice and the love of God. You should have done these and not left the others undone. Woe to you Pharisees, because you love the best seats in the synagogues and respectful greetings in the marketplaces. Woe to you because you are like hidden graves which men walk over without knowing it."

One of the experts in the law answered him. "Teacher, when you say these things, you insult us also."

Jesus replied, "You experts in the law, woe to you also, because you load people down with burdens that are difficult to carry and you yourselves will not lift a finger to help them. Woe to you, because you build tombstones for the prophets, and it was your fathers who killed them. This means that you approve of what your fathers did: they killed the prophets, and you built their tombs. Because of this, God in his wisdom said, 'I will send them prophets and apostles, some of whom they will kill and others they will persecute.' Therefore, this generation will be held responsible for the blood of all the prophets that has been shed since the beginning of the world; from the blood of Abel to the blood of Zechariah, who perished between the altar and the sanctuary. Yes, I tell you, it will be required of this generation. Woe to you experts in the law because you have taken away the key to knowledge; you yourselves have not entered and yet have hindered others from doing so."

When Jesus went outside, the Pharisees and teachers of the law opposed him fiercely and besieged him with questions. trying to catch him in something he might say.

4

The Storyteller

Parable of the Sower

Parable of the Weeds

The Treasure and the Pearl

The Dragnet

The Mustard Seed and the Leaven

Calming of the Storm

A Demon-Possessed Man

Jesus Brings Back a Dead Girl
      and Cures a Woman with a Hemorrhage

Death of John the Baptist

Jesus Feeds Five Thousand

Jesus Walks on Water

More Pharisees with Questions

Parable of the Great Banquet

Nicodemus

The Cost of Being a Disciple

Parable of the Lost Sheep

The Good Shepherd

Parable of the Prodigal Son

Faith of the Canaanite Woman

The Samaritan Woman at the Well

The Crippled Man at the Sheep Pool

Parable of the Sower: Luke 8:1–15

*J*esus travelled from town to town, proclaiming the good news of the kingdom of God. The twelve were with him, and some women provided support for them out of their own means. One of these women was Mary—called Magdalene—from whom seven demons had been driven out; another was Joanna, the wife of Chuza, the manager of Herod's estate; and another was Susanna, along with many others.

After a large crowd gathered and people from many towns came to hear him, Jesus told the following parable. "A farmer went out to sow seed. As he was scattering the seed, some of it fell on the path, where it was trampled on, and the birds ate it; some fell on rocky ground where there was little soil and it withered away. Other seed fell among thorns, which grew and choked the plants. Finally, a portion of it fell on good ground, where it yielded a crop a hundred times the amount of seed that was sown. Let everyone take heed of what you hear."

His disciples asked him the meaning of this parable.

Jesus said, "The knowledge of the kingdom of God has been given to you, but to others I speak in parables; that 'seeing they may not see, and hearing they may not understand.' The meaning of the parable is this: The seed is the word of God. Those that fell on the path are people who hear the word of God, and the devil comes along and takes away the word from their hearts so that they may not believe and be saved. Those on rocky ground are the ones who hear the word with joy, but because they have no root, they believe for a while but eventually fall away. The seed that fell among thorns represents those who hear the word but go on their way through life and the riches and pleasures and worries of their world prevent them from maturing. The seed on good soil are those with a noble and a good heart, hear the word, hold it tightly, and bring forth fruit with patience."

Parable of the Weeds: Matthew 13:24–50

Jesus proposed another parable: "The kingdom of heaven is like a man who sowed good seed in his field. When everyone was asleep, his enemy came and scattered darnel weeds through the crop. When the crop began to mature, the weeds appeared as well. The owner's servants came to him and said, 'Did you not sow good seed in your field? Where did this darnel come from?'

"The owner replied, 'An enemy has done this.'

"His servants said to him, 'Do you want us to go out and pull the weeds up?'

"He replied, 'No, you might also take the wheat along with the darnel; let them grow together until harvest. I will then tell the reapers to first gather the weeds and bind them up for burning and then gather the wheat into my barn.'"

He explained to his disciples the meaning of this parable: "The farmer sowing the seed is the Son of Man, the good seed, the children of the kingdom and the weeds, children of the evil one, and the enemy who sowed them is the devil. The reapers are angels, and they will collect the weeds and burn them with fire, along with all things that cause stumbling and those who do iniquity. There will be weeping and gnashing of teeth The righteous who have been faithful to the Son of Man will shine like the sun in their Father's kingdom. This is how it will be at the end of the world."

The Treasure and the Pearl: Matthew 13:45–46

"The kingdom of heaven is like a merchant seeking fine pearls and having found a pearl of great price, goes and sells all he had and buys it."

The Dragnet: Matthew 13:47–50

"The kingdom of heaven is also like a dragnet cast into the sea which collected fish of every kind, and when it was full was dragged up on to the beach. They sorted out what was good and put it into containers; the rest they threw away. This is how it will be at the end of the world: angels will separate the wicked from the righteous and throw them in the furnace of fire, where there will be weeping and gnashing of teeth."

The Mustard Seed and the Leaven: Luke 13:18–21; Luke 8:19–21

"The kingdom of heaven is like a grain of mustard seed, which is one of the smallest seeds of all, and someone planted it in the garden. It grew and became one of the larger garden plants, and the birds came and built their nests in its branches. Similarly, it is like yeast, which a woman took and kneaded into three measures of flour, until it was all leavened."

When Jesus finished these parables, he moved on from that district, travelling to other towns and villages. The crowds continued to follow him, and he performed many miracles. His mother and brothers came to see him as they were concerned about him. Not being able to go in and see him because of the crowds, they had someone give him a message: "Your mother and brothers are outside wanting to see you."

He replied, "My mother and brothers are those who hear God's word and put it into practice."

Calming of the Storm: Luke 8:22–25

One day he said to his disciples, "Let us go over to the other side of the lake."

They got into a boat and set out. As they sailed, he fell asleep. A storm came down the lake, and the boat was being buffeted by fierce winds; they were taking on dangerous amounts of water.

They woke him, saying, "Master, Master, we're going to drown!"

He got up and rebuked the wind and the raging waters; they ceased, and all was calm. He asked his disciples, "Where is your faith?"

In fear and amazement, they asked one another, "Who is this? He commands even the winds and water, and they obey him."

A Demon-Possessed Man: Luke 8:26–39

They sailed to the region of the Gadarenes, which is across the lake of Galilee. When Jesus stepped ashore, a demon-possessed man from the tombs came toward him; for a long time, he hadn't worn clothes and was unable to be restrained—he even snapped the chains used to fetter him. When he saw Jesus, he ran up to him, shouting, "What do you want with me, Jesus, Son of the Most High God? Don't torment me."

Jesus was commanding the unclean spirit to come out of the man; he said, "Come out of him, unclean spirit! What is your name?"

"Legion," he replied, "for there are many of us." They begged Jesus repeatedly not to send them into the abyss.

A large herd of pigs was feeding on the mountainside, and the demons asked Jesus if they could go into them. He allowed them to enter the pigs. At that they went into the pigs, and the whole herd rushed down the mountain and into the lake and drowned. When those tending the pigs saw this, they rushed off and told it in the city and country.

People went out to see what happened. When they arrived, they saw the man who had been possessed, now fully clothed and in his right mind, sitting at Jesus's feet. When everybody who found out how the demon-possessed man had been cured and what had happened to the pigs, they asked Jesus to depart from them, for they were very much afraid.

As Jesus was leaving in the boat, the man begged to go with him, but Jesus said to him, "Go to your house and declare what great things God has done for you."

So, the man went off and proclaimed to everyone throughout the country what great things Jesus had done for him.

Jesus Brings Back a Dead Girl and Cures a Woman with a Hemorrhage: Luke 8:40–56

When Jesus returned, a crowd was expecting him. A man named Jairus, a synagogue leader, came and fell at Jesus's feet and begged him to come to his house, because his only daughter, a girl of about twelve, was dying.

As Jesus was on his way, the crowd was pressing against him. In the crowd was a woman who had been having an issue with bleeding for twelve years and no one had been able to cure her. She came up behind him and touched the hem of his cloak, and her bleeding stopped immediately.

"Who touched me?" Jesus asked.

When no one said anything, Peter said, "Master, the people are crowding and pressing against you."

But Jesus said, "Someone touched me; I know the power has gone out from me."

Then the woman, seeing that she could not go unnoticed, came trembling and fell at his feet. In the presence of all, she told why she had touched him, and she had been healed immediately.

Then he said to her, "Daughter, your faith has made you well. Go in peace."

While Jesus was speaking, someone came from Jairus's house and said, "Your daughter is dead; don't trouble the teacher anymore."

Hearing this, Jesus said to Jairus, "Don't be afraid; just believe and she will be healed."

When he arrived at Jairus's house, he did not let anyone go inside with him except Peter, John, and James, and the father of the child and her mother. The people were weeping and mourning for her.

Jesus said, "Stop weeping. She is not dead, but asleep."

They ridiculed him, knowing she was dead. But he took her by the hand and said, "My child, get up."

Her spirit returned, and she stood up. Jesus told her parents to give her something to eat. They were amazed, but he commanded them to tell no one what had been done.

Death of John the Baptist: Matthew 14:1–13

It was around this time that Herod was being pestered by Herodias, who had been his brother Phillip's wife, to do something about John the Baptist. She wanted Herod to have him killed, because he didn't consider it lawful for them to live together. Herod wouldn't do it for fear of the people, who regarded John as a prophet.

On Herod's birthday, Herodias's daughter danced before the court, which delighted Herod so much that he swore an oath that he would give her anything she wanted. Prompted by her mother, she said, "Give me, here on a platter, the head of John the Baptizer." Because he had sworn the oath, and because of the guests who were present, Herod ordered it to be given, and he went and beheaded John in Prison. His head, brought in on a platter, was given to the young girl, and she brought it to her mother.

John's disciples buried his body and informed Jesus. When Jesus heard this, he withdrew from there by boat to a deserted place.

Jesus Feeds Five Thousand: Matthew 14:13–21

The people heard where he had gone and followed him from the cities on foot. When he saw such a great multitude, he had compassion for them and healed their sicknesses.

When evening had come, the disciples came to him and said, "This place is deserted, and the hour is already late. Send the multitude away so that they can go into the towns and villages to buy themselves food."

He replied, "They don't need to go away. You give them something to eat."

They answered, "All we have is five loaves of bread and two fish."

Jesus replied, "Bring them here to me."

He commanded the multitude to sit down on the grass, and he took the five loaves and two fish. Looking up to heaven, he blessed them and broke them and then gave them to his disciples, and the disciples gave it to the multitude. They all ate and were filled. They collected twelve basketsful of that which remained left over. Those who ate were about five thousand men, besides women and children.

Jesus Walks on Water: Matthew 14:22–33

Immediately afterward, Jesus made the disciples get into the boat and cross over the lake, while he sent the multitude away. Then he went up the mountain by himself to pray there alone. By now it was evening, and the boat was in the middle of the sea, distressed by waves, for the wind was contrary.

On the fourth watch of the night, Jesus came to them, walking on the sea. When the disciples saw him, they were troubled, saying, "It is a ghost!"

But immediately Jesus spoke to them, saying, "Cheer up! It is I! Don't be afraid."

Peter spoke up and said, "Lord, if it is you, tell me to come to you across the water."

Jesus said, "Come!"

Peter stepped out of the boat and started walking toward Jesus; when he realized how strong the wind and waves were, he became frightened and began to sink. He called out, "Lord, save me!"

Jesus stretched out his hand and took hold of him, saying, "You of little faith, why did you doubt?"

When they had climbed back into the boat, the wind died down and it was calm again. Those in the boat came and worshiped him, saying," You are truly the Son of God."

After making the crossing, they came to the land of Gennesaret. When the people of that place recognized him, they sent into the surrounding regions and brought to him all who were sick. They begged him that they might just touch the fringe of his garment. As many as touched it were made whole.

More Pharisees with Questions: Matthew 15:1–9; Luke 14:7–14

Jesus and his disciples were invited eat with one of the elders. The Pharisee and scribes came to Jesus from Jerusalem saying, "Why do your disciples disobey the traditions of the elders?"

Jesus said, "Why do you disobey the commandment of God for the sake of your tradition? For God has said, 'Honor your father and mother,' and he who speaks evil of father or mother, let him be put to death. But you say, 'Whoever may tell his father or his mother, "Whatever help you might otherwise have gotten from me is a gift devoted to God,"' and so he does not honor his father or mother. For the sake of your traditions, you have made the commandment of God void. You hypocrites! Well did Isaiah prophesy about you, saying,

'These people draw near me with their mouth, and honor me with their lips, but their heart is far from me. In vain do they worship me, teaching as doctrine rules made by men.'"

Elsewhere, Jesus noticed how the guests picked the places of honor at the table, so he told them this parable: "When someone invites you to a wedding feast, do not take the place of honor, for a person more honorable than you may have been invited. The host who invited both of you will come to you and say, 'Give this person your seat,' then in shame you will have to take a lower place. When you are invited, take the lowest place so that when your host comes, he will say to you, 'Friend, move up higher.' Then you will be honored in the presence of all who sit at the table. For all those who exalt themselves will be humbled, and those who humble themselves will be exalted."

Then Jesus said to his host, "When you give a dinner or supper, don't invite your friends or brothers or rich neighbors, for they will probably invite you back and repay you. Instead, invite the poor, the crippled, the lame, and the blind, and you will be blessed. Although they can't repay you, you will be repaid at the resurrection of the righteous."

Parable of the Great Banquet: Luke 14:15–24

When one of those at the table heard this, he said to Jesus, "Blessed is the one who will feast in the kingdom of God."

Jesus replied, "A certain man was preparing a great supper and invited many guests. When it was ready, he sent out his servants to tell all those who had been invited, 'Come, for everything is now ready.'

"They all as one began to make excuses.

"The first said, 'I have just bought a field and must go and see it, please excuse me.'

"Another said, 'I have just bought five yoke of oxen and I'm on my way to try them out, please excuse me.'

"Still another said, 'I just got married and can't come.'

"The servants came back and reported these things to their master. The owner of the house became very angry and ordered his servants, 'Go into the streets and lanes of the town and bring in the poor, the maimed, the blind, and the lame.' The servants did this, but there was still room.

"The master then told them, 'Go out into the highways and hedges and compel them to come so that my house will be full. I tell you not one of those who were invited will get a taste of my supper!'"

Nicodemus: John 3:1–21

A certain Pharisee named Nicodemus, who was a ruler of the Jews, came to Jesus at night and said to him, "Rabbi, we know you are a teacher come from God, for no man can do the signs that you do unless he is with God."

Jesus gave him this answer: "No one can see the kingdom of God unless he is born from above."

Nicodemus said, "How can a man be born again when he is old? Can he return to his mother's womb and be born all over again?"

Jesus replied, "I can assure you; no one can enter God's kingdom without being born of water and Spirit. Flesh begets flesh, Spirit begets Spirit. Don't be surprised when I tell you, you must all be born again from above."

"How can these things be?" Nicodemus asked.

Jesus responded, "You hold the office of teacher of Israel and do not understand these things. We talk about what we know and testify to what we have seen, but you do not accept our witness. If I tell you about earthly things and you don't believe, how can you believe if I tell you heavenly things? God so loved the world that he gave his only Son that whoever believes in him will have eternal life. God did not send his Son to condemn the world but that the world should be saved through him. Whoever believes in him should not perish but have eternal life. This is the judgement; the light came into the world. But men loved the darkness rather than the light for their works were evil. He who acts in truth stays in the light so that all his deeds can be clearly seen."

The Cost of Being a Disciple: Luke 14:25–35

At another time later, large crowds were again following Jesus. He turned to them and said, "If anyone comes to me and is not prepared to forsake father and mother, wife and children, brothers, and sisters, even his own life, he can't be my disciple, and neither can anyone who doesn't bear his own cross.

"If one of you wants to build a tower, won't you first sit down and count the cost to see if you have enough to finish it? If you lay the foundations and are unable to finish it, everyone who sees it will mock you, saying. 'This man began to build and was unable to finish.' What king is about to go to war against another king? Won't he first sit down and consider whether he is able, with ten thousand men, to oppose the one coming against him with twenty thousand? If he is not able, he will send an envoy while the other is still a long way off and ask for conditions of peace. In the same way, those of you who do not renounce all you have cannot be my disciples. Salt is good, but if it becomes flat and tasteless, how can it become salty again? It is fit neither for the soil nor for the manure pile. It is thrown out and trampled on. Listen carefully to what you are hearing!"

Parable of the Lost Sheep: Luke 15:1–7

In the crowd were many tax collectors and sinners, and the Pharisees noticed how Jesus welcomed them all. They muttered, "This man welcomes sinners and eats with them."

Aware of their murmurings, Jesus related this parable: "Which of you men, if he had a hundred sheep and lost one, wouldn't leave the ninety-nine in safe, open country and go after the lost sheep until he found it? And when he has found it, he joyfully puts it on his shoulders and goes home. He calls together his neighbors and friends and says to them, 'Rejoice with me, for I have found my lost sheep.' I tell you that in the same way there will be more rejoicing in heaven over one sinner who repents than over ninety-nine righteous persons who do not need to repent."

The Good Shepherd: John 10:1–21

"Anyone who does not enter the sheep pen by the gate, but enters in some other way, is a thief. The true shepherd enters by the gate, and he calls his sheep and, recognizing his voice, they follow him out. His sheep trust him for they know his voice,but not a stranger."

Jesus used this figure of speech, but no one understood what he was saying, so he said again, "I am the sheep's door; all who came before me are thieves and robbers, but the sheep didn't listen to them. If anyone enters in by me, he will be saved, and will go in and out and find pasture. I came that they may have life and have it abundantly. I am the good shepherd, who lays down his life for his sheep. The hired hand doesn't own the sheep and when the wolf comes, he runs away, and the wolf attacks the flock and scatters it. I am the good shepherd; I know my sheep and they know me, just as I know my Father and he knows me, and I lay down my life for the sheep. There are other sheep, not of this fold, that I must bring in also; they will hear my voice and there shall be one flock and one shepherd. The reason my Father loves me is because I lay down my life and I lay it down by myself. I received this command from my Father."

Those who heard these words were confused and divided among themselves.

Parable of the Prodigal Son: Luke 15:11–32

Jesus continued: "A certain man had two sons. The younger one said, 'Father, give me my share of your property.' So, he divided his livelihood between them. Not many days after, the younger son gathered all his shares and travelled to a far country. There he wasted his property with riotous living. When he had spent all of it, a severe famine arose in that country, and he began to be in need. So, he went and joined one of the citizens of that country, who sent him out into the fields to feed the pigs. He didn't have anything to eat, and he wanted to fill his belly with the husks that the pigs were eating. When he came to his senses, he said, 'How many of my father's hired servants have bread enough to spare? Here I am dying with hunger. I will get up and go to my father and say to him: "Father, I have sinned against heaven and you; I am no longer worthy to be called your son; make me like one of your hired servants."'

"So, he got up and came to his father. While he was still a long way off, his father saw him and was filled with compassion for him; he ran to his son, threw his arms around him, and kissed him. The son said to him, 'Father I have sinned against heaven and against you. I am no longer worthy to be called your son.'

"But the father said to his servants, 'Quick, bring the best robe and put it on him. Put a ring on his finger and sandals on his feet. Bring in the fattened calf and kill it. Let's have a feast and celebration, for this son of mine was dead and is alive again, was lost and is found.' They began to celebrate.

"Now his older son was out in the fields, and when he came near the house, he heard music and dancing. He called one of the servants and asked him what was going on. 'Your brother has come,' he replied, 'and your father has killed the fatted calf because he has him back safe and healthy.' The older brother became angry and would not go in, so his father went out and begged him. But he answered his father, 'All these years I have served you and never disobeyed a command of yours; yet you never even gave me a young goat so I could celebrate with my friends. But this son of yours who has devoured your property with prostitutes comes home, and you kill the fatted calf for him!'

"'My son,' the father said, 'you are always with me and everything I have is yours. It was appropriate to celebrate and be glad because the brother of yours was dead and is alive again. He was lost and is found.'"

Faith of the Canaanite Woman: Matthew 15:21–28

Jesus continued to visit other towns and villages where he cured many of their illnesses and drove out unclean spirits; people were amazed to see the deaf hear, the blind see, and the lame walk again.

He then withdrew to the seaside district around Tyre and Sidon. It happened that a Canaanite woman was there anc cried out to him, "Have mercy on Lord, Son of David, my daughter is in terrible trouble and is tormented by a demon."

He gave her no word of response. His disciples came up to him and begged him "send her away; for she cries after us."

Jesus replied, "I wasn't sent to anyone but the lost sheep of the house of Israel."

But she came forward then and worshipped him, saying, "Help me, Lord."

But he answered, "It is not right to take the children's bread and throw it to the dogs."

"Please, Lord," she insisted, "even the dogs eat the crumbs that fall from the master's table."

Jesus then said, "Woman, you have great faith; be it done to you even as you desire."

And her daughter was healed from that hour.

The Samaritan Woman at the Well: John 4:1–42

Samaritan woman at the well
Courtesy of the lumoproject.com

As he was going to Galilee, he had to pass through Samaria and came to the Samaritan town called Sychar. Jacob's well was there and Jesus, tired by the journey, sat by the well. It was about the sixth hour when a Samaritan woman came to draw water. Jesus asked her for a drink.

She said, "How is it that you, being a Jew, ask for a drink from me, a Samaritan woman?" (For Jews have no dealings with Samaritans.)

Jesus replied, "If only you knew the gift of God and who it is who is asking you for a drink, you would have asked, and he would have given you living water."

"Sir, you have nothing to draw with and the well is deep, so how could you give this living water? Are you a man greater than our father, Jacob, who gave us this well?"

Jesus replied, "Whoever drinks the water that I give will never be thirsty again, and it will become in him a well of water, springing up to eternal life."

She said, "Sir, give me some of this water so that I may not have to keep coming here to draw."

Jesus said, "Go and call your husband and bring him here."

"I have no husband," she replied.

Jesus said, "You are right when you say you have no husband, for you have had five husbands; the one with whom you are living now is not your husband. This you have said truly."

"I perceive that you are a prophet, sir," the woman said. "Our fathers worshipped on this mountain, and yet you Jews say that it is in Jerusalem that people ought to worship."

Jesus said, "The hour is coming when you will worship neither on this mountain nor in Jerusalem. The hour is here already when true worshippers will worship the Father in spirit and in truth. God is Spirit, and those who worship him must worship in spirit and truth."

The woman said to him, "I know that the Messiah is coming and that he will tell us everything."

Jesus said, "**I who speak to you am he.**"

At this point his disciples returned and were surprised to find him talking to the woman; but no one asked, "What do you want from her?" or "Why are you talking with her?"

Leaving her water jar, the woman went back to the town and said to the people, "Come, see a man who told me everything I ever did. Could this be the Messiah?"

They came out of the town and started walking toward him.

Then his disciples urged him, "Rabbi, eat something."

But he said to them, "I have food to eat that you know nothing about."

Then his disciples said to each other, "Could someone have brought him food?"

Jesus said to them, "My food is doing the will of him who sent me and to finish his work. Don't you have a saying: 'It's still four months until harvest'? I tell you, open your eyes and look at the fields; they are white for harvest already. Even now the one who reaps draws a wage and harvests a crop for eternal life so that the sower and the reaper may both rejoice together. Hence, the saying, 'One man sows and another reaps,' is true. I sent you to reap what you had not worked for; others have done the hard work, and you have reaped the benefit of their labor."

Many of the Samaritans from that town believed in him because of the word of the woman, and when they came to him, they urged him to stay with them; he stayed two days. And because of his words, many more became believers. They said to the woman, "We no longer believe just because of what you told us; now we have heard for ourselves, and we know that this man really is the Savior of the world."

The Crippled Man at the Sheep Pool: John 5:1–15

After two days he left for Galilee, even though he had pointed out that a prophet has no honor in his own country. Nevertheless, they welcomed him because of the things they had seen him do at a Passover festival in Jerusalem, which they had attended.

One of these things he did happened near the Sheep Gate (which in Aramaic is called Bethesda), where there is a pool surrounded by five porticos that shelters numerous sick, lame, blind, and people with all kinds of ailments, waiting for the moving of the water. One who was there had been an invalid for thirty-eight years.

When Jesus saw him lying there and knew he had been sick for a long time, he asked him, "Do you want to get well?"

"Sir," the invalid replied, "I have no one to help me into the pool when the water is stirred. While I am trying to get in, someone else goes down ahead of me."

Then Jesus said to him, "Arise! Take up your mat and walk."

At once the man was cured; he picked up his mat and walked.

The day this took place was a Sabbath, and some of the Jewish leaders said to the man, "This is the Sabbath, and the law forbids you to carry your mat."

He replied, "The man who made me well told me to pick up my mat and walk."

They said to him, "Who is this person who told you to do this?"

The man who was cured had no idea who it was, for Jesus had withdrawn into the crowd.

Later, Jesus found him in the temple and said to him, "See? You are well again. Sin no more so that nothing worse happens to you."

The man went away and told the Jewish leaders that it was Jesus who had made him well again.

5

Conflict with the Teachers of the Law

Testimonies about Jesus: John 5:31–47; 5:19–30

The Pharisees challenged him: "Here you are appearing as your own witness; your testimony is not valid."

Jesus replied, "If I were to testify about myself, my witness is not valid; there is one who testifies about me: you have sent to John, and he has testified to the truth. I mention this so that you may be saved; John was a lamp that produced bright light and for a time you were willing to rejoice in his light. I have testimony greater than that of John. The works that the Father has given me to finish, those that I am doing now, testify that my Father has sent me.

"You search the Scriptures because in them you think you have eternal life. These are the very Scriptures that testify about me, yet you will not come to me that you may have life. I know that you do not have the love of God in yourselves. I have come in my Father's name and you don't receive me, but if someone else comes in his own name, you do receive him. How can you receive glory that comes from one another, but do not seek the glory that comes from the only God?

"Do not think that I will accuse you before the Father; your accuser is Moses on whom your hopes are set. If you really believed Moses, you would believe me, for he wrote about me. But if you don't believe what he wrote, how are you going to believe my words?"

Then they asked him, "Where is your father?"

Jesus replied, "You do not know me or my Father."

This made them even more antagonistic since he was now calling God his own Father, making himself equal with God.

Jesus gave them this answer: "The Son can do nothing by himself but what he sees the Father doing. The Father loves the Son and shows him all he does and will show even greater works that you may marvel. The Father raises the dead to life as does the Son; the Father judges no one and has given all judgment to the Son, so that all may honor the Son even as they honor the Father.

"I tell you, whoever hears my words and believes him who sent me has eternal life already. The time has come when the dead will hear the voice of the Son of God and live, for the Father has life in himself, he gave to the Son to have life in himself. Even those who are in their tombs will hear his voice and come out, those who have done what is good, to the resurrection of life; and those who have done evil to the resurrection of judgment. I do not seek my own will but the will of my Father who sent me."

Jesus Heals an Official's Son: John 4:43–54

There was a certain nobleman whose son lay sick at Capernaum, and when he heard that Jesus had come out of Judea into Galilee, he went and begged him to come and heal his son, who was close to death.

Jesus said to him, "Unless you people see signs and wonders, you will never believe."

The nobleman said, "Sir, come down before my child dies."

Jesus replied, "Go your way; your son lives."

The man believed the word that Jesus spoke to him and went his way. While he was still on the way, his servants met him and told him: "Your child lives."

When he asked them at what time this had happened, they told him, "Yesterday, at the seventh hour, the fever left him."

The father realized that this was the exact time that Jesus had said to him, "Your son lives."

So, he and his whole household came to believe.

Jesus went to the synagogue, and the crowds found him there. Many of them had been present when he fed the five thousand.

The Bread of Life: John 6:25–58

"You are not looking for me because you have seen signs, but because you ate of the loaves and were filled. Don't work for food which perishes, but for the food which remains to eternal life, food that the Son of Man will give you, for on him God the Father has set his seal."

Then they asked him, "What must we do to do the work God requires of us?"

Jesus answered, "The work of God is this: that you believe in him whom he has sent."

They asked him, "What sign will you give us so that we may believe you? Our ancestors ate the manna in the wilderness; as it is written, 'He gave them bread from heaven to eat.'"

Jesus said to them, "It was not Moses who gave your fathers bread from heaven. It is my Father who gives you the true bread from heaven; for the bread of God is the bread that comes down from heaven and gives life to the world."

"Sir," they said, "always give us this bread."

Jesus declared, "I am the bread of life. Whoever comes to me will never go hungry and whoever believes in me will never be thirsty. You have seen me and still do not believe; whoever comes to me I will never drive away. It is my Father's will that I shall lose none of those he has given me but raise them up on the last day."

At this they began to grumble. "He said, 'I am the bread of life that came down from heaven,' but we know him as Jesus, whose father and mother we know."

Jesus said, "Don't murmur among yourselves; no one comes to me unless the Father draws them to me; it is written in the prophets: 'They will be taught by God.' I am the bread of life; your fathers ate manna in the wilderness, yet they died, but here is the bread that came down from heaven that anyone can eat and not die. This bread is my flesh, which I will give for the life of the world."

They contended with one another, saying, "How can this man give us his flesh to eat?"

Jesus responded, "I tell you this: unless you eat the flesh of the Son of Man and drink his blood, you shall not have life in you. Whoever eats my flesh and drinks my blood has eternal life and I will raise him up on the last day. Whoever eats my flesh and drinks my blood, remains in me and I in them and they will live forever."

Many Disciples Desert Jesus: John 6:60–71

On hearing this, many of the disciples said, "This is a hard saying. Who can listen to it?"

Aware of the grumbling, Jesus said, "Does this cause you to stumble? Then what if you see the Son of Man ascend to where he was before? The Spirit gives life; the flesh counts for nothing. **The words I have spoken to you are Spirit.** But some of you still don't believe."

Jesus knew from the beginning which of them did not believe and who would betray him; he went on to say, "This is why I told you that no one can come to me unless it is given to him by my Father."

From this time many disciples turned back and no longer followed him.

Jesus asked the twelve, "You don't want to go away too, do you?"

Simon Peter said, "Lord, to whom shall we go? You have the word of eternal life. We have come to believe and know that you are the Holy One of God."

Jesus replied, "Have I not chosen you twelve? Yet one of you is a devil."

The Man Blind from Birth: John 9:1–41

As Jesus was leaving after the festival, he saw a man blind from birth.

His disciples asked him, "Rabbi, who sinned, this man or his parents that he was born blind?"

Jesus replied, "Neither this man nor his parents, but that the works of God might be revealed in him. I must do the work of him who sent me while it is day. The night is coming when no one can work. While I am in the world, I am the light of the world."

After saying this, he spat on the ground, made some mud with the saliva, and anointed the man's eyes, saying, "Go and wash in the pool of Siloam."

The man went and washed and came back seeing.

His neighbors and those who knew that he was blind before said, "Isn't this he who sat and begged?"

Others said, "No, he only looks like him."

But the man himself insisted, "I am that man."

They asked him, "How were your eyes opened?"

He replied, "A man they call Jesus made some mud, anointed my eyes, and said to me, 'Go to the pool of Siloam and wash.' So, I went and washed, and I received sight."

"Where is this man?" they asked him.

"I don't know," he said.

They brought him to the Pharisees. It was a Sabbath when Jesus made the mud and opened his eyes. Again, the Pharisees asked him how he received his sight.

He said to them," He put mud on my eyes, I washed, and I see."

Some of the Pharisees said, "This man is not from God for he does not keep the Sabbath."

Others said, "How can a man who is a sinner do such signs?" So, they were divided.

They asked the blind man again, "What do you say about this man, because he opened your eyes?"

The man replied, "He is a prophet."

They refused to believe the man and sent for his parents and asked them," Is this your son who was born blind? How does he now see?"

The parents said, "We know he is our son and that he was born blind; how he now sees, we don't know. Ask him what happened; he is of age." They said these things because they knew that anyone who confesses that Jesus was the Messiah would be put out of the synagogue.

They called the man again and said, "Give glory to God. We know that this man is a sinner."

He replied, "I have already told you what happened, but you did not listen. I don't know if he is a sinner. All I know is I was blind and now I see. Do you want to hear it again so you can become his disciples too?"

"We know God spoke to Moses, but we don't know where this man comes from," they said.

The man replied," You don't know where he comes from, yet he opened my eyes, and nobody has ever heard of a man born blind having his eyes opened. If the man were not from God, he could do nothing like this."

To this they replied, "You were altogether born in sin, and do you teach us?" They threw him out of the synagogue.

Jesus heard what they had done, and when he found him, he said, "Do you believe in the Son of God?"

"Who is he?" the man asked. "Tell me so that I may believe in him."

Jesus said, "You have now seen him; it he who now speaks with you. I came into the world for judgment that those who don't see may see and those who see may become blind."

Some Pharisees who were nearby heard this and said, "What, are we blind too?"

Jesus replied, "If you were blind, you would have no sin, but now that you claim you can see, your sin remains."

On another occasion he was moving around the district of the Ten Cities. People brought the sick to lay before him, wherever he was. They laid them in villages, in towns, at crossroads, and in the marketplaces and begged him to let them just touch his coat. All who touched him were cured.

Healing of the Deaf Mute: Mark 7:31–37

Some people brought him a deaf man who had a speech impediment. Jesus took him aside from the crowd. He put his fingers in the man's ears and then spat and touched the man's tongue.

He looked up to heaven, and with a deep sigh said to him, "*Ephphatha*!" This means *be opened*.

At this the man's ears were opened, and the impediment in his tongue was released and he began to speak plainly. Jesus asked them not to talk about it, but the more he asked, the more widely they proclaimed it.

Peter's Declaration: Matthew 16:13–20; John 21:14–18

Jesus and his disciples continued in the villages around Caesarea Philippi and on the way, he asked them, "Who do men say that I am?"

They replied, "Some say John the Baptist; others say Elijah; and still others, Jeremiah or one of the prophets."

"But what about you? Who do you say I am?"

Peter answered, "You are the Messiah, the Son of the living God."

Jesus replied, "Blessed are you, Simon, son of Jonah, for flesh and blood did not reveal this to you, but my Father in heaven. And I tell you that you are Peter, and on this rock I will build my church, and the gates of hades will not prevail against it. I will give you the keys of the kingdom of heaven. Whatever you bind on earth will be bound in heaven, and whatever you release on earth will be released in heaven."

Then Jesus said to Peter, "Now Simon, son of Jonah, do you love me?"

"You know I love you, Lord," Peter replied.

Jesus said, "Feed my lambs."

Jesus asked Peter again, "Simon, son of Jonah, do you love me more than these?"

Peter was hurt because he had asked him again and said, "Lord, you know everything and know well that I love you."

Jesus said to him, "Feed my sheep. As a young man, you went about as you pleased, but when you are older, you will stretch out your hands and be carried off against your will."

Then he commanded his disciples not to tell anyone that he was the Messiah.

Jesus Predicts His Death: Matthew 16:21–23

From then on, Jesus began to tell his disciples that he must go to Jerusalem and suffer many things at the hands or the elders, the chief priests, and scribes; he must be killed, and on the third day be raised to life.

Peter said, "Far be it from you, Lord. This will never be done to you."

Jesus turned to him and said, "Get behind me, Satan; you are a stumbling block to me, for you are not setting your mind on the things of God but on the things of men."

The Transfiguration: Matthew 17:1–9

About a week after this conversation, Jesus took Peter, James, and John with him and went up on to a high mountain to pray.

As he was praying, the appearance of his face changed and shone like the sun and his garments became as white as light. Suddenly, Moses and Elijah appeared talking with him.

Peter said to him, "Lord, is it good for us to be here? If you want, let us make three tents: one for you, one for Moses, and one for Elijah."

While he was speaking, a bright cloud overshadowed them. A voice came out of the cloud, saying, "This is my beloved Son, on whom my favor rests. Listen to him."

When the disciples heard it, they fell on their faces and were very afraid.

Jesus came and touched them and said, "Get up and don't be afraid."

They looked around and saw Jesus alone. They kept all this to themselves and didn't tell anyone what they had seen.

Jesus Heals a Demon-Possessed Boy: Matthew 17:14–21

The next day when they came down from the mountain, a large crowd met him.

A man in the crowd called out, "Lord, I beg you, have mercy on my son, for he is epileptic and suffers grievously, for he often falls into the fire and often into the water. I brought him to your disciples, and they could not cure him."

Jesus said, "Faithless and perverse generation! How long will I be with you? Bring the boy here."

Jesus rebuked the spirit, and it came out of the boy, and he was cured from that hour. The disciples asked Jesus why they could not expel it.

Jesus said, "Because of your unbelief, this kind does not leave but by prayer and fasting."

Second Prophecy of the Passion: Matthew 17:22–23; 18:1–7

While everyone was marveling at all Jesus did, he said to his disciples, "Listen carefully to what I am about to tell you: the Son of Man is going to be delivered into the hands of men."

They didn't understand what this meant and were afraid to ask him about it.

An argument broke out among them as to who was greatest in the kingdom of heaven.

Knowing their thoughts, Jesus called a little child and had him stand among them. He said, "Unless you become as little children, you will in no way enter the kingdom of heaven. Whoever receives one such little child in my name receives me. It is the one who is least among you who will be the greatest. Whoever causes one of these little ones who believes in me to stumble, it would be better that he has a millstone tied around his neck and be drowned in the depths of the sea."

Fraternal Correction: Matthew 18:21–32; 15–17; 23–35

Then Peter came and asked him, "Lord, when my brother sins against me, how often shall I forgive him? Until seven times?"

Jesus replied, "I don't tell you until seven times but until seventy times seven. If he has sinned against you, go to him alone and show him his fault; if he doesn't listen, take one or two more with you as witnesses that every word may be established. If he refuses to listen to them, tell it to the assembly. If he refuses to hear the assembly also, let him be to you as a Gentile or a tax collector.

"The kingdom of God is like a certain king who wanted to reconcile accounts with his servants. One was brought to him who owed him ten thousand talents, but because he couldn't pay, his lord commanded that he be sold along with his wife and children and all that he had and payment to be made.

"The servant fell down and kneeled before him saying, 'Lord, have patience with me and I will repay you all.' Moved with compassion, the lord of the servant released him and forgave him the debt.

"When that same man went out, he met a fellow servant who owed him one hundred denarii, and he grabbed him and took him by the throat saying, 'Pay me what you owe.' When he couldn't, he had him thrown into prison until he should pay back that which was due.

"When the other servants saw this, they went and reported the whole thing to their lord. His lord called him in and said to him, 'You wicked servant, I forgave you all your debt because you begged me. Shouldn't you also have had mercy on your fellow servant, just as I had mercy on you?' His lord was angry and delivered him to the tormentors until he should repay all that was due to him.

"My heavenly Father will do the same to you if you don't each forgive your brother from your heart for his misdeeds."

The Question of Divorce: Mark 10:2–10; Luke 20:27–38

Some Pharisees came up to him and said, to test him, "Is it lawful for a man to divorce his wife for any reason?"

He replied, "Haven't you read that he who made them from the beginning made them male and female? For this cause, a man shall leave his father and mother and shall join his wife, and the two shall become one flesh. They are no longer two, but one flesh. What, therefore, God has joined together, let no man tear apart."

They said, "Then why did Moses allow a certificate of divorce to be written, and to divorce her?"

Jesus replied, "It was because of hardening of your hearts that Moses let you divorce, but at the beginning it was not like that. I say to you now, whoever divorces his wife, except for sexual immorality, and marries another commits adultery, and he who marries her when she is divorced commits adultery."

His disciples said, "If that is the case between man and wife, it is better not to marry."

Jesus replied, "Not all men can accept this teaching."

Some Sadducees, including those who deny there is a resurrection, then said, "Teacher, Moses wrote to us: 'If a man's brother dies having a wife but is childless, the brother takes the wife and raise the children for his brother.' Now there were seven brothers; the first one married a woman and died childless. The second married her and so on to the seventh, leaving no children. At the resurrection, whose wife will she be?"

Jesus replied, "The people of this age marry and are given in marriage. Those who are worthy of taking part in the age to come will neither marry nor be given in marriage, for they become like angels. They are children of God, being children of the resurrection, and even Moses showed that the dead rise, for he calls the Lord 'The God of Abraham, the God of Isaac, and the God of Jacob.' He is not the God of the dead, but of the living, for all are alive to him."

Whose Son Is the Messiah? Luke 20:41–44

Jesus then said to them, "Why is it said that the Messiah is the Son of David? David himself says in the book of psalms: 'The Lord said to my Lord, "Sit at my right hand, until I make your enemies the footstool for your feet.' David calls him Lord, so how can he be his son?"

They were unable to answer, and no one dared ask him any more questions.

The Danger of Riches: Luke 18:18–30

Another time a man came up to him and said, "Good teacher, what shall I do to inherit eternal life?"

"Why do you call me good? No one is good except God. You know the commandments: 'Don't commit adultery,' 'Don't murder,' 'Don't steal,' 'Don't give false testimony,' 'Honor your father and your mother.'"

The young man said, "I have observed these things from my youth up."

Jesus answered, "You still lack one thing. Sell all you have and distribute it to the poor. You will have treasure in heaven. Then come, follow me."

When the young man heard this, he went away sad, because he was very rich.

Jesus, seeing that he had become very sad, said, "It is hard for those who have riches to enter the kingdom of God; it is easier for a camel to go through the eye of a needle than for a rich man to enter into the kingdom of God."

Those who heard it said, "Then who can be saved?"

Jesus said, "The things that are impossible with men are possible with God."

Peter said, "We have left everything and followed you."

Jesus replied, "There is no one who has left house or wife, or brother, or parents, or children, for the sake of the kingdom of God, who will not receive many times more in this time, and in the world to come, eternal life."

The Rich Man and Lazarus: Luke 16:19–31

"There was a rich man who was dressed in purple and fine linen and lived in luxury every day. At his gate lay a beggar named Lazarus, covered in sores, and he desired to be fed with the crumbs that fell from the rich man's table. Even the dogs came and licked his sores.

"It happened that the beggar died, and he was carried away by the angels to Abraham's bosom. The rich man also died and was buried. In hades, being tormented, he lifted up his eyes and saw Abraham far off, and Lazarus at his bosom. He called to him, 'Father Abraham, have mercy on me and send Lazarus that he may dip the tip of his finger in water and cool my tongue, for I am in anguish in this flame.'

"But Abraham said, 'Remember that you in your lifetime received good things while Lazarus received bad things. Now here he is comforted, and you are in anguish. Between all this, between us and you there is a great gulf fixed, that those who want to pass from here to you are not able and that none may cross over from there to here.'

"He said, 'Then I ask you, father, that you would send him to my father's house, for I have five brothers, that he may testify to them so that they won't come into this place of torment.' "Abraham replied, 'They have Moses and the prophets; let them listen to them.'

"'No, Father Abraham,' he replied. 'If one from the dead goes to them, they will repent.'

"He said to him, 'If they do not listen to Moses and the prophets, they will not be persuaded, even if one rises from the dead.'"

Parable of the Rich Fool: Luke 12:13–21

Someone in the crowd said to him, "Teacher, tell my brother to divide the inheritance with me."

Jesus replied, "Man, who made me a judge or arbitrator over you? Watch out! Keep yourselves from covetousness, for a man's life doesn't consist of the abundance of things he possesses."

He spoke a parable to them, saying, "The ground of a certain rich man brought forth abundance. He reasoned, 'I don't have enough room to store my crops.' So he said, 'I will pull down my barns and build bigger ones to store all my grain and my goods. Then I will have plenty to last me for years and will be able to take my ease, eat, drink, and be merry.'

"But God said to him, 'You foolish man, tonight your soul is required of you. Who will get what you have prepared for yourself?'

"This is how it will be for those who lay up treasure for themselves and are not rich toward God."

6

Storytime

The Use of Parables: Luke 8:9–10

esus taught the people using parables as they were better able to relate things to their everyday lives. The stories were meaningful, and the familiarity of what they heard helped them understand the messages being conveyed.

The disciples asked, "Why do you speak to them in parables?"

"To you it is given to know the mysteries of the kingdom of God, but to the rest in parables; that 'seeing they may not see, and hearing they may not understand.'"

Parable of the Shrewd Manager: Luke 16:1–15

He said to his disciples, "There was a rich man who had a manager. An accusation was made to him that this man was wasting his possessions. He called him and said, 'What is this that I hear about you? Give an account of your management, for you can no longer be my manager if what I hear is true.'

"The manager considered, 'What will I do? My lord is taking away my management position. I don't have strength to dig, and I am ashamed to beg. I will call all my lord's debtors and see if I can plan so they may receive me into their houses when I am no longer manager.'

"He called in each one of his lord's debtors. He asked the first, 'How much do you owe my lord?' He replied, 'A hundred gallons of olive oil.' The manager told him, 'Take your bill and write fifty.' He asked the second debtor how much he owed, and he told him, 'Six hundred bushels of wheat.' The manager told him to make it three hundred.

"His lord commended the dishonest manager because he had done wisely, for the children of this world are, in their own generation, wiser than the children of the light. However, if you have not been faithful in that which is another's, who will give you that which is your own? No one can serve two masters. Either you will hate one and love the other or hold on to one and despise the other. You cannot serve both God and money."

Parable of the Bags of Gold: Matthew 25:14–30

"The kingdom of heaven is like a man going into another country, who called in his servants and entrusted his goods to them. To one he gave five bags of gold, to another, two bags and to yet another, one bag each according to his own ability. Then he went on his journey.

"The one who had the five bags went and traded with them and made another five. In the same manner, he who got the two gained another two. The one who received the one bag went and dug in the earth and hid his lord's money.

"After a long time, the lord of those servants returned and reconciled accounts with them. The servant who had received the five bags brought in the other five and said, 'Lord, you delivered me five bags, and I have gained five beside them.' His lord replied, 'Well done, good and faithful servant; because you have been faithful with a few things, I will set you over many. Enter the joy of your lord.' The same thing happened with the servant who had received the two bags.

"The third servant who had received the one bag came in and said, 'I knew you were a hard man, reaping where you did not sow and gathering where you did not scatter. I was afraid and hid your gold in the earth. Here is what is yours.'

"His lord answered, 'You wicked and slothful servant, you could have deposited it with the bankers, and at my coming I should have received it back with interest. Take the bag of gold from him and give it to the one who has ten bags. For whoever has will be given more, and they will have an abundance. But from him who doesn't have, even that will be taken away. Throw out the unprofitable servant into the outer darkness, where there will be weeping and gnashing of teeth.'"

The Sheep and the Goats: Matthew 25:31–46

"When the Son of Man comes in his glory, and all his angels with him, he will sit on the throne of his glory. Before him all the nations will be gathered, and he will separate them one from another, just as a shepherd separates the sheep from the goats, with the sheep on his right and the goats on his left. Then the King will say to those on his right, 'Come, you who are blessed by my Father, inherit the kingdom prepared for you from the foundation of the world. For I was hungry, and you gave me food to eat, thirsty and you gave me drink, was a stranger and you took me in. I was naked and you clothed me, was sick and you cared for me; I was in prison, and you came to me.'

"Then the righteous will answer, saying, 'Lord, when did we do any of these things for you?' The King will reply, 'Whatever you did for one of the least of these my brothers, you did it to me.'

"Then he will say to those on the left, 'Depart from me, you who are cursed, into the eternal fire prepared for the devil and his angels, for you did nothing for me when I was in need. Whatever you did not do for one of the least of these, you didn't do it to me.' Then they will go away to eternal punishment' but the righteous to eternal life."

The Laborers in the Vineyard: Matthew 20:1–16

"The kingdom of heaven is like a landowner who went out early in the morning to hire laborers to come and work in his vineyard. He agreed to pay them a denarius for the day and sent them into his vineyard. He went out at about the third hour and saw others standing idle in the marketplace. He said to them, 'You also go out and work in my vineyard, and I will pay you whatever is right.' He went out at noon and at the ninth hour did likewise. About the eleventh hour, he found others standing around and said, 'Why do you stand here all the day idle?'

"'Because no one has hired us,' they said.

"He said to them, "you also go into my vineyard, and you will receive whatever is right.'

"When evening came, the lord of the vineyard said to his manager, 'Call the laborers and pay them their wages, beginning from the last to the first.' The workers who started at the eleventh hour each received a denarius. Those who were hired first supposed they would receive more but only received a denarius. They began to murmur against the master, saying, 'These who were hired last only worked for an hour and you have made them equal to us who have borne the burden of the day and the scorching heat!'

"He answered, 'Friend, I am doing you no wrong. Didn't you agree to work for a denarius? I want to give the one who was hired last the same as I gave you. It is lawful for me to do what I want with what I have. Or is your eye evil, because I am good? So, the last will be first, and the first last. For many are called, but few are chosen."

Jesus Sends Out the Seventy: Luke 10:1–22

After this, Jesus appointed seventy others and sent them two by two ahead of him, saying, "The harvest is plentiful, but the laborers are few. Pray therefore to the Lord of the harvest, that he may send out laborers. I am sending you out like lambs among wolves. Whoever listens to you listens to me; whoever rejects you rejects me and therefore rejects he who sent me."

Sometime later when they returned, they said with joy, "Lord, even the demons are subject to us in your name."

He replied, "I saw Beelzebub falling like lightning from heaven. I have given you authority to tread on serpents and scorpions and to overcome all the power of the enemy; nothing will harm you. However, don't rejoice that the spirits are subject to you, but rejoice that your names are written in heaven."

Jesus, full of joy through the Holy Spirit, said, "I thank you, Father, Lord of heaven and Earth, because you have hidden these things from the wise and learned and revealed them to little children; for so it was well pleasing in your sight. All things have been delivered to me by my Father. No one knows who the Father is except the Son, and no one knows who the Son is except the Father and those to whom the Son desires him to be revealed."

Parable of the Good Samaritan: Luke 10:25–37

An expert in the law wanted to test Jesus, so he asked him, "What must I do to inherit eternal life?"

Jesus answered, "What is written in the law? How do you read it?"

He answered, "Love the Lord your God with all your heart and with all your soul and with all your strength and your entire mind; love your neighbor as yourself."

"You have answered correctly; do this and you will live," Jesus replied.

But he wanted to justify himself, so he asked Jesus, "And who is my neighbor?"

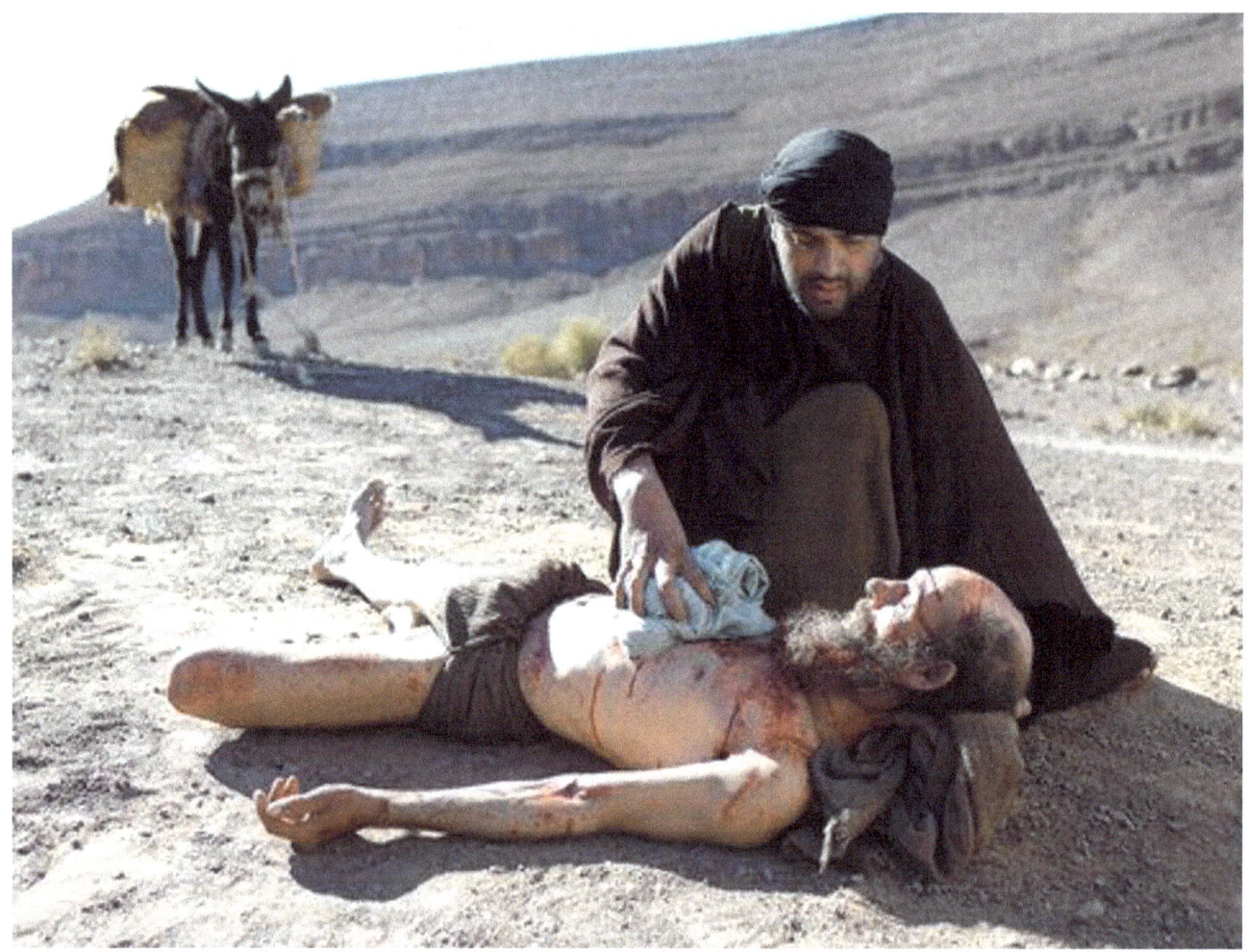

The good Samaritan
Courtesy of the lumoproject.com

In reply Jesus said, "A man was going down from Jerusalem to Jericho. He fell among robbers, who stripped him and beat him and departed, leaving him half dead. A priest was going down that way, and when he saw the man, he passed by on the other side. In the same way, a Levite also, when he came to the place and saw him, passed by on the other side of the road. But when a Samaritan came to where the man was, he was moved with compassion and bound up his wounds, pouring on oil and wine. He set him on his own donkey and took him to an inn and took care of him. The next day, he took out two denarii and gave them to the host and said to him, 'Take care of him. Whatever you spend beyond that, I will repay you when I return.' Which of these three do you think was a neighbor to the man?"

The expert in the law replied, "He who showed mercy on him."

Jesus told him, "Go and do likewise."

Jesus's Teaching about Prayer: Luke 11:1–13; Matthew 6:5–15

Jesus used often to go to lonely places to pray and one day, when he had finished, his disciples asked him to teach them how to pray also. He said to them, "When you pray, say,

> Father in heaven,
> Holy is your name.
> May your kingdom come.
> Your will be done on earth, as it is in heaven.
> Give us each day our daily bread.
> Forgive us our debts, as we forgive our debtors.
> Lead us not into temptation,
> But deliver us from the evil one."

Then Jesus said to them, "Suppose you have a friend, and you go to him at midnight and ask him, 'Friend, lend me three loaves of bread, for someone has come to visit me from a journey, and I have nothing to set before him.'

"Suppose the one inside says, 'Don't bother me. The door is shut, and my children and I are in bed. I can't get up and give it to you'? However, when you ask again, he gets up and gives it to you, not because of your friendship but because of your persistence.

"I tell you, keep asking and it will be given to you. Keep seeking, and you will find. Keep knocking, and the door will be opened for you.

"Which of you fathers, if your son asks you for bread, will give him a stone. If he asks for a fish, will give him a snake? If you, who are evil, know how to give good gifts to your children, how much more will your Father in heaven give the Holy Spirit to those who ask him?"

The Pharisee and the Tax Collector: Luke 18:9–14

To some who felt superior in their own righteousness, Jesus told this parable: "Two men went up to the temple to pray: one a Pharisee and the other a tax collector. The Pharisee stood in full view by himself and prayed, 'God, I thank you that I am not like the rest of men, extortioners, unrighteous, adulterers, or even like this tax collector. I fast twice a week and give a tithe of all I get.' But the tax collector, standing far away, wouldn't even lift his eyes to heaven but beat his breast, saying, 'God, be merciful to me, a sinner!' I tell you that this man, rather than the other, went down to his house justified before God. For everyone who exalts himself will be humbled, but he who humbles himself will be exalted."

Parable of the Persistent Widow: Luke 18:1–8

Then Jesus told his disciples a parable to show them that they should always pray and never give up. He said, "There was a judge who didn't fear God or care what people thought. In the same city there was a widow who often came to him, saying, 'Defend me from my adversary.' For some time, he wouldn't, but afterward he said to himself, 'Though I neither fear God nor respect man, but because this widow bothers me, I will defend her or else she will wear me out by her continual coming.'

"Listen to what the unrighteous judge says. Won't God avenge his chosen ones, who cry out to him day and night? Yet he exercises patience with them. Will he keep putting them off? He will avenge them quickly. However, when the Son of Man comes, will he find faith on the earth?"

The Ten Lepers: Luke 17:11–19

On his way to Jerusalem, along the border between Samaria and Galilee, he was about to enter a village when ten men with leprosy called out to him, "Jesus, Master, have mercy on us!"

When he saw them, he said, "Go, show yourselves to the priests."

As they went along, they were cleansed. One of them, a Samaritan, when he saw that he was healed, came back and threw himself at Jesus's feet and thanked him.

Jesus asked, "Weren't ten cleansed? Where are the other nine? Were there none found who returned to give glory to God, except this stranger? Get up and go your way; your faith has healed you."

The Narrow Door: Luke 13:22–27

Jesus went through the towns and villages, teaching as he made his way to Jerusalem. Someone asked him, "Lord, are only a few to be saved?"

He said to them: "Strive to enter through the narrow door. Many will seek to enter and will not be able. Once the master of the house gets up and has shut the door, you will stand outside and knock saying, "Lord, lord, open to us.' And he will answer, 'I don't know you or where you come from. Depart from me all you workers of iniquity.'"

At the Home of Martha and Mary: Luke 10:38–42

They came to a village where a woman named Martha received him into her house. She had a sister called Mary, who sat at Jesus's feet, listening to what he said. Martha was distracted with much serving, and she came to Jesus and said, "Lord, don't you care that my sister has left me to serve alone? Ask her to help me!"

Jesus answered, "Martha, Martha, you are anxious and troubled about many things, but one thing is needed. Mary has chosen the good part, which will not be taken away from her."

At the home of Martha and Mary
Courtesy of thr lumoproject.com

Jesus Teaches at the Festival: John 7:10–24; 8:12–24; 8:30–59.

The disciples went up to Jerusalem to the Festival of Tabernacles, and Jesus followed some days later as he wanted to be as anonymous as possible. During the festival, the Jews were looking for him, wondering where he was; some said, "He is a troublemaker who is misleading the crowd," while others said, "He is a good man." Halfway through the festival, Jesus went into the temple and began to teach. The Jews said, "How did this man get such learning without having been taught?"

Jesus answered, "My teaching is not my own but his who sent me. If anyone desires to do his will, he will know about the teaching, whether it is from God or if I am speaking from myself. Moses has given you the law, yet not one of you keeps it; he gave you circumcision, which you sometimes perform on a Sabbath so that the law of Moses may not be broken. Are you angry with me because I made a man completely healthy on the Sabbath? Stop judging by appearances but judge righteous judgment.

"I am the light of the world; he who follows me will not walk in the darkness but will have the light of life. I am going away, and you will seek me, and you will die in your sins. Where I am you cannot come. You are from beneath; I am from above. I said therefore to you that you will die in your sins, for unless you believe that I am he, you will die in your sins.

"If you remain in my word, then you are truly my disciples. You will know the truth, and the truth will make you free."

They retorted, "We are Abraham's seed and have never been in bondage to anyone, so how do you say, 'You will be set free'?"

Jesus answered, "Everyone who commits sin is the slave of sin; that is why if the Son sets you free, you will really be free. I know you are Abraham's seed, yet you seek to kill me because my word finds no place in you. I say the things that I have seen with my Father, and you also do the things that you have seen with your father. If you were Abraham's children, you would do the work of Abraham. I am telling you the truth, which I have heard from God, and you want to kill me.

"Abraham did nothing like that. It was God who sent me here and you cannot bear to hear my words, because the father you spring from is the devil, who brought death to man from the beginning and doesn't stand in the truth. Because I tell the truth, you don't believe me. Can any one of you convict me of sin? If a man keeps my words, he will never see death. Abraham rejoiced that he would see my day."

At that, the Jews objected: "You are not yet fifty; how could you have seen Abraham?"

Jesus answered, "Before Abraham came into existence, I AM."

At that they picked up rocks to stone him, but he was hidden from them and went away out of the temple and back across the Jordan to where John had formerly been baptizing.

Paying Taxes: Matthew 22:15–22; 17:24–27

They were trying to trap Jesus, so they said to him, "Teacher, we know you are an honest man and that you teach the way of God in truth. You aren't partial to the opinion of others, so is it lawful to pay taxes to Caesar or not?"

Jesus was aware of their wickedness and said to them, "You hypocrites! Why are you trying to test me? Show me the tax money.

They brought him a denarius, and he asked them, "Whose is this image and inscription?"

"Caesar's," they said.

So, Jesus said to them, "Give to Caesar the things that are Caesar's and to God the things that are God's."

When they heard it, they marveled and left him and went away.

Later, when they came to Capernaum, they came to Peter and said, "Doesn't your teacher pay the temple tax?"

Then he turned to Peter and said, "What do you think, Simon? From whom do the kings of the earth receive toll or tribute? From their children or from strangers?"

"From strangers," Peter answered.

Jesus said to him, "Lest we cause offense, go to the sea, and with the first fish you catch, open its mouth and you will find some coins. Take them and pay for my tax and yours."

Watchfulness: Luke 12:1–8; 22–34; 35–40

In the meantime, a crowd had begun to gather, and Jesus told them, "Beware of the yeast of the Pharisees, which is hypocrisy. There is nothing covered up that will not be revealed nor hidden that will not be known.

"Do not be afraid of those who kill the body and after that can do no more. The one you should fear is he who, after your body has been killed, has power to throw you into hell.

"Aren't five sparrows sold for two pennies? Yet not one of them is forgotten by God. Indeed, the very hairs in your head are numbered; don't be afraid, you are worth more than many sparrows.

"Whoever publicly acknowledges me before others, the Son of Man will acknowledge before the angels of God."

They continued moving from town to town and village to village around Galilee, and he healed all who came to him with all sorts of ailments.

Jesus then told them, "Don't be anxious for your life; which of you by worrying can add a single cubit to your height? Don't seek what you will eat or what you will drink; your Father knows you need these things. Make for yourselves purses that don't grow old, a treasure in the heavens that doesn't fail and where no thief approaches or moth destroys. For where your treasure is, there will your heart be also.

"Be dressed ready for service and keep your lamps burning so that when your lord returns and knocks, you will immediately be able to open the door for him. It will be good for those servants whose lord finds them watching when he comes, even if he comes in the middle of the night or toward daybreak. Therefore, be ready also, for the Son of Man is coming in an hour that you don't expect."

Parable of the Ten Virgins: Matthew 25:1–13

Jesus continued with the theme of readiness with this parable:

> "The kingdom of heaven will be like ten virgins who took their lamps and went out to meet the bridegroom. Five of them were foolish, and five were wise. The foolish ones took their lamps, but no extra oil; the wise ones took oil in their vessels with their lamps.
>
> Now while the bridegroom delayed, they all slumbered and slept. At midnight there was a cry. "Behold, the bridegroom is coming, come out to meet him." Then all those virgins arose and trimmed their lamps. The foolish said to the wise, "Give us some of your oil for our lamps are going out."
>
> But the wise answered, saying, "What if there isn't enough for us and you? You go rather to those who sell and buy for yourselves." While they went away to buy, the bridegroom came, and those who were ready went in with him to the marriage feast, and the door was shut.
>
> Afterward, the other virgins also came, saying, "Lord, lord, open to us." But he answered, 'Most certainly I tell you, I don't know you.' Watch, therefore, for you don't know the day, nor the hour, in which the Son of Man is coming."

The Coming of the Kingdom: Luke 12:49–53; 21:12–15; 17:20–25

"I came to throw fire on the earth. I wish it were already kindled. Do you think I can have come to give peace on earth? No, I tell you, I bring division. From now on there will five in one household divided against each other two against three: father against son, mother against daughter.

"They will seize you, persecute you, and put you in prison and you will be brought before magistrates on account of my name. Don't worry about what you will say in your defense, for I will give you words and wisdom that no one will be able to contradict.

"The coming of the kingdom of God is not something that can be observed; people won't be saying, 'Here it is,' or 'there it is,' because the kingdom of God is in your midst. The day of the Son of Man will be like the lightning that flashes and lights up the sky from one end to the other. But first he must suffer many things and be rejected by this generation."

Repent or Perish: Luke 13:3–9

"Unless you repent, you will all perish."

He spoke this parable. "A man had a fig tree growing in his vineyard and went to look for fruit on it but didn't find any. He said to the vine dresser, 'For three years now I have been looking for fruit on this tree but haven't found any. Cut it down! Why does it waste good soil?'

"'Sir,' the man replied, 'leave it for one more year and I will dig around it and fertilize it. If it bears fruit next year, fine! If not, after that you can cut it down.'"

Prophecy of the Passion: Matthew 20:17–19

Jesus took the twelve aside and told them, "We are going up to Jerusalem, and the Son of Man will be delivered over to the chief priests and scribes, and they will condemn him to death, and will hand him over to the Gentiles to be mocked and scourged and crucified. On the third day he will be raised up."

The disciples did not understand, as the meaning was hidden from them.

The Mother of James and John: Matthew 20:20–28

The mother of the sons of Zebedee came up to him with her sons, and kneeling, wanted to ask a favor.

He said, "What is it you want?"

She said, "Command that these sons of mine will sit, one on your righthand side and the other on your left, in your kingdom."

In reply Jesus said, to the sons, "You don't know what you are asking; can you drink of the cup I am about to drink, and be baptized with the baptism that I am baptized with?"

"We can," they said.

He told them, "You will indeed drink from my cup and be baptized with the baptism I am baptized with but to sit at my right or left is not mine to give; but it is for whom it has been prepared by my Father."

When the ten heard this, they were indignant with the two brothers

Jesus called them together and said, "The rulers of nations lord it over them. It shall not be so among you. Whoever wants to rank first among you, must serve the needs of all. The Son of Man has come, not to be served by others but to serve; to give his life as a ransom for many."

Bartimaeus Receives His Sight: Luke 18:35–43

As Jesus approached Jericho, a blind man by the name of Bartimaeus was sitting by the roadside, begging. When he heard that the crowd was following Jesus, he shouted out in a loud voice, "Jesus, Son of David, have mercy on me." Many rebuked him, but he shouted all the louder, "Son of David, have mercy on me."

Jesus stopped and commanded him to be brought to him. Jesus asked him, "What do you want me to do for you?"

The blind man said, "Lord, that I may see again."

Jesus said, "Receive your sight; your faith has healed you."

Immediately, he received his sight and followed Jesus along the road, glorifying God.

Zacchaeus the Tax Collector: Luke 19:1–10

Jesus entered Jericho and was passing through. A man by the name of Zacchaeus was the chief tax collector there and was very rich. He was trying to see Jesus, and because he was only short, he couldn't see over the crowd, so he ran on ahead and climbed a sycamore tree so he could see.

When Jesus reached the spot, he looked up and said to him, "Zacchaeus, hurry and come down, I must stay at your house today." He came down and received him joyfully. All the people saw this and said, "He has gone to lodge with a man who is a sinner."

Zacchaeus stood up and said, "Lord, I give half of my possessions to the poor and if I have wrongfully exacted anything of anyone, I restore four times as much."

Jesus said to him, "Today, salvation has come to this house, because this man too is a son of Abraham. For the Son of Man came to seek and to save that which was lost."

7

To Jerusalem

The Raising of Lazarus

Meeting of the Sanhedrin

Anointing at Bethany

Triumphant Entry into Jerusalem

Lament over Jerusalem

Eviction of the Temple dealers

The Widow's Offering

Farewell Discourses

The Vine and the Branches

Rejection by the World

The Work of the Holy Spirit

Jesus's Departure

The Raising of Lazarus: John 11:1–44

artha, Mary, and their brother Lazarus were close friends with Jesus. They lived at Bethany, just outside Jerusalem.

While Jesus was in Galilee, Lazarus became very ill and the sisters sent word: "Lord, the one you love is very sick."

When he heard this news, he said, "This sickness will not end in death, but for the glory of God, that the Son of God may be glorified by it."

Now Jesus loved Martha and her sister and Lazarus, but he stayed where he was for two more days before saying to his disciples, "Let us go back to Judea again."

The disciples told him, "The Jews were just trying to stone you, and are you going there again?"

Jesus answered, "Our friend Lazarus has fallen asleep, but I am going there to awaken him."

The disciples thought he was talking about natural sleep, so Jesus told them plainly, "Lazarus is dead, and for your sake, I'm glad I was not there so that you may believe. Nevertheless, let's go to him."

Now Thomas, also known as Didymus, said to his fellow disciples, "Let us also go, that we may die with him."

When Jesus came, he found that Lazarus had already been in the tomb for four days. Now Bethany was only about two miles from Jerusalem and many people had come out from there to comfort Martha and Mary in the loss of their brother.

When Martha heard that Jesus had come, she went out to meet him, but Mary stayed in the house.

"Lord," Martha said, "if only you had been here, my brother wouldn't have died. But I know that even now, God will give you whatever you ask."

Jesus said to her, "Your brother will rise again."

Martha answered, "I know he will rise again in the resurrection at the last day."

Jesus said to her, "I am the resurrection and the life. The one who believes in me will still live, even if he dies. Whoever lives and believes in me will never die. Do you believe this?"

"Yes, Lord," she replied. "I believe that you are the Messiah, the Son of God who is to come into the world."

After she said this, she went back and called her sister, Mary, aside. "The teacher is here and is asking for you."

When Mary heard this, she got up quickly and went to him. When those with Mary saw how quickly she got up, they followed her out, assuming she was going to the tomb to mourn.

When Mary reached Jesus, she fell at his feet and said, "Lord, if you had been here, my brother wouldn't have died."

When Jesus saw her weeping, along with those with her, he was deeply moved in spirit and troubled. He asked, "Where have you laid him?"

"Come and see, Lord," they replied.

And Jesus wept.

The Jews said, "See how he loved him." Some said, "Could not he have kept this man from dying?"

Jesus, once more deeply moved, came to the tomb; it was a cave with a stone laid across the entrance. He said, "Take away the stone."

"But Lord," Martha said, "by this time there is a bad odor. He has been there four days."

Jesus said, "Didn't I tell you that if you believe, you will see the glory of God?"

They took away the stone. Jesus looked up and said, "Father, I thank you that you have heard me; I know that you always hear me, but I say this because of the people standing here, so that they may believe that you sent me."

When he said this, Jesus called out in a loud voice, "Lazarus, come out!"

The dead man came out, his hands and feet wrapped with strips of linen, and a cloth around his face. Jesus said to them, "Free him and let him go."

Meeting of the Sanhedrin: John 11:45–54

Many of those who saw what Jesus did came to believe in him; some others went to the Pharisees to report all that had happened.

The chief priests and Pharisees then called a council and said, "What are we to do with this man performing all these signs? If we leave him alone like this, everyone will believe in him, and the Romans will come and take away both our place and our nation."

At that point, the high priest, Caiaphas, addressed them. "You know nothing at all, nor do you consider that it is advantageous for us that one man should die for the people and that the whole nation should not perish."

From that day onward they took counsel that they might put him to death. Jesus therefore walked no more openly among the Jews and departed from there to a city called Ephraim and stayed there with his disciples.

Anointing at Bethany: John 12:1–11; Matthew 26:10–13

Sometime later, the Passover was at hand and Jesus and his disciples wert to Bethany to the home of Martha, Mary, and Lazarus, who were having a celebration. While they were reclining at the table, Mary brought in a jar of ointment of pure nard, very precious, and anointed the feet of Jesus, and wiped his feet with her hair. The house was filled with the fragrance of the ointment.

Judas Iscariot, who kept the finances, said, "Why wasn't this expensive ointment sold for three hundred denarii and the money given to the poor?"

Jesus replied, "Leave her alone; she has kept this for the day of my burial. The poor you always have with you, but you won't always have me. Wherever in the world the Gospel is preached, what she has done will be told in remembrance of her."

Triumphant Entry into Jerusalem: Luke 19:29–44; John 12:12–15; Matthew 21:9–11

The next day, Jesus was going up to Jerusalem for the festival, and as he drew near to Bethpage and Bethany, at the Mount of Olives, he sent off two of his disciples, saying, "Go to the village ahead of you, and as you enter it you will find a colt tied there whereon no man has yet sat. Untie it and bring it here, and if anyone asks you why you are untying it, say, 'The Lord needs it.'"

They went and found it just as he had told them and brought it back. They threw their cloaks on to the colt and set Jesus on it.

Thus, was fulfilled what was written:

Don't be afraid, daughter of Zion
Your king comes to you,
Sitting on a donkey's colt.

As he went along, the people spread their cloaks on the road, while some cut branches from the trees and lay them along his path. The whole assembly began joyfully to praise God for all the miracles they had seen and cried out in loud voices, "Blessed is the King who comes in the name of the Lord. Peace in heaven and glory in the highest."

Some of the Pharisees in the crowd said, "Teacher, rebuke your disciples."

He said, "I tell you, if they keep quiet, the stones will cry out."

Lament over Jerusalem: Luke 19 41–44; Mark 13:1–2

As he approached Jerusalem, he wept over it, saying, "If you only had known today the things that belong to your peace! But now they are hidden from your eyes. The days will come when your enemies will throw up a barricade against you, surround you, hem you in on every side, and dash you and your children within you to the ground. They will not leave in you one stone on another, because you didn't know the time of your visitation."

Eviction of the Temple Dealers: John 2:13–22; Matthew 21:12–13

Jesus entered the temple precincts and drove out all those engaged in buying and selling. He overturned the tables of the money changers and the stalls of the dove sellers, saying to them, "Scripture has it: 'My house is a house of prayer,' but you are turning it into a den of robbers."

With that, he left them and went out of the city and went to Bethany, where he spent the night. In the morning, as he was returning to the city, he felt hungry, and seeing a fig tree by the roadside, he went over to it and found no fruit but just leaves.

He said, "Let there be no fruit from you forever."

The tree withered up and the disciples were dumbfounded when they saw it. They asked, "Why did the tree wither so quickly?"

Jesus answered, "Believe me, if you have faith and don't doubt, not only will you do what I did to the fig tree, even if you told this mountain, 'Be taken up and cast into the sea,' it would be done. All things, whatever you ask in prayer, believing, you will receive."

Every day he was teaching in the temple, and even though the Pharisees and teachers of the law were there, they were unable to do anything about him, because the people were believing him.

The Widow's Offering: Luke 21:1–4.

As Jesus looked up, he saw the rich putting their gifts into the temple treasury. He also saw a poor widow put in two small coins and said, "Truly I tell you; this poor widow has put in more than all these others; they put in gifts for God out of their abundance, but she, out of her poverty, all she had to live on."

Farewell Discourses: John 13:36; 14:1–7

One time his disciples came to him, and Peter said, "Lord, where are you going?"

Jesus answered, "Where I am going you can't follow now but you will follow afterward. Don't let your hearts be troubled; believe in God and have faith in me. In my father's house there are many dwelling places, and I am going to prepare a place for you, and I will come back and take you with me. You know the way that leads where I go. **I am the way, the truth, and the life**. No one comes to the Father except through me; if you had known me, you would have known my Father also. From now on, you know him and have seen him. I will pray to the Father and will ask him to give you another counsellor to be with you always; the Spirit of truth, whom the Father will send in my name, will teach you all things and will remind you of all the things I said to you."

The Vine and the Branches: John 15:1–16

"I am the vine and my Father is the farmer. He takes away every branch that doesn't bear fruit, but the branches that bear fruit, he prunes that they may bear more. You are already pruned clean, because of the words I have spoken to you. Remain in me as I do in you. A branch can't bear fruit of itself unless it remains in the vine, neither can you unless you remain in me. I am the vine, and you are the branches; he who remains in me, and I in him, will bear much fruit.

"A man who does not live in me is thrown out as a withered branch to be picked up and thrown in the fire. But if my word remains in you, you will ask whatever you desire, and it will be done for you. My Father has been glorified in your bearing much fruit and so you will be my disciples. As the Father has loved me, so I have loved you; you will remain in my love if you keep my commandments. All this I tell you that my joy may be yours and your joy may be complete. This is my commandment: love one another as I have loved you.

"There is no greater love than to lay down one's life for one's friends. You are my friends since I made known to you all that I heard from my Father. It was not you who chose me, but I chose you to go forth and bear fruit, so that all you ask the Father in my name he will give to you."

Rejection by the World: John 15:19–25

"If the world hates you, know that it hated me before you; if you were of the world, the world would love its own. But because you are not of the world, since I chose you out of the world, it hates you. Remember when I told you, 'A servant is not greater than his lord,' so they will treat you just as they treated me for my name's sake, for they do not know the one who sent me.

"If I had not come and spoken to them or performed such works as have never been seen before, they would not have sinned, but now they have no excuse for their sin. They go on hating me and my Father and this fulfils the text, 'They hated me without cause,' as written in their law."

The Work of the Holy Spirit: John 14:30–31; 16:1–11

"I will no longer speak much with you for the prince of this world comes and he has nothing in me. He has no hold on me, but the world must know that I must do what the Father has commanded me. It is to your advantage that I go away for if I don't go the Counsellor won't come to you.

"The Father will send the Holy Spirit in my name and will instruct you in everything and remind you of all that I told you. 'Peace' is my farewell gift to you; this is not the peace that the world gives, but the peace from my Father.

"The Spirit of truth will guide you to all truth; it will prove the world wrong about sin, about righteousness and about judgement. About sin, because they don't believe in me, about righteousness, because I am going to my Father, about judgment, because the prince of this world has been judged."

Jesus's Departure: John 16:19–33; 12:35–50

"In a little while, you won't see me, but soon after that you will see me again. You will weep and mourn while the world rejoices; you will be sorrowful, but your sorrow will turn to joy. When a woman gives birth, she is concerned that her time has come. But when she has delivered the child, she no longer remembers her anguish, for the joy that a child has been born into the world. Therefore, you now have sorrow, but I will see you again and your hearts will rejoice, and no one will take your joy away from you. I leave the world and go to the Father.

"The time has come when each of you will be scattered each to his own place and will leave me alone. Yet I am not alone, my Father is with me. I have told you these things so that in me you may have peace. In this world you will have oppression but have courage! I have overcome the world. For a little while the light is with you. Walk while you have the light that darkness doesn't overtake you. He who walks in the darkness doesn't know where he is going. While you have the light, believe in the light, that you may become children of the light. If anyone listens to my voice and doesn't believe it, I don't judge him. I came not to judge the world but to save it. I have done all the Father has commanded me and his commandment means eternal life."

There were many, even among the Sanhedrin, who believed in him, but they refused to admit it for fear of being ejected from the synagogue.

8

Trials and Tribulation

Judas Agrees to Betray Jesus

The Last Supper

Prayer for the Disciples

At Supper

Jesus Predicts His Betrayal

Peter's Denial Foretold

The Agony in the Garden

The Arrest

Before the Sanhedrin

Peter's Denial

The End of Judas

Before Pilate and Herod

The Crucifixion

The Death of Jesus

The Burial

Judas Agrees to Betray Jesus: Luke 22:1–6; Matthew 26: 14-16.

The chief priests and scribes sought how they might put him to death, for they feared the people. Then one of the twelve—Judas Iscariot—went to the chief priests and asked, "What are you willing to give me if I deliver him over to you?" They counted out thirty pieces of silver, and from then on Judas watched for an opportunity to hand Jesus over.

The Last Supper: Luke 22:7–22; Matthew 26:14–21; John 13:3–9

On the first day of the Festival of Unleavened Bread, the disciples came to Jesus and asked, "Where do you want us to make preparations for you to eat the Passover?"

He replied, "Go into the city, and a man carrying a jar of water will meet you; follow him to the house that he enters, and say to the owner: the teacher says, 'My appointed time is near; where is the guest room where I may keep the Passover with my disciples?'"

The disciples did as Jesus commanded and prepared the Passover. When evening came, Jesus was sitting at the table with them. He rose, took off his cloak, and wrapped a towel around him. Then he poured water into a basin, washed the disciples' feet, and dried them with the towel.

Peter said, "Lord, are you going to wash my feet?"

Jesus answered, "You may not realize now what I am doing, but later you will understand."

Peter answered, "You shall never wash my feet!"

Jesus replied, "Unless I wash you, you have no part with me."

Then Peter said, "Lord, not just my feet but my hands and head as well."

Jesus said, "Those who have bathed need only to wash their feet and they are completely clean. You are all clean, though not every one of you."

He knew who was going to betray him. He returned to the table and continued: "You call me Teacher and Lord, and so I am, What I have done for you is set you an example and do to one another as I have done to you. If you know these things, blessed are you if you do them."

Jesus then offered this prayer:

Prayer for the Disciples: John 17:1–26

"Father, the hour has come; glorify your Son that he may glorify you. You have granted him authority to give eternal life to all those you have given him; eternal life is to know you, the only true God. I pray for these you have given me for they are really yours. These are in the world as I come to you. Holy Father, keep them through your name, which you have given me. While I was with them in the world, I kept careful watch, and not one of them was lost except the one who was lost to fulfil the scriptures. I say this while I am still in the world so they may share my joy in full. I gave them your word, and the world has hated them for it, because they are not of this world, but I ask you to keep them from the evil one. I sanctify myself now for their sakes that they may be sanctified in truth.

"My prayer is not for them alone; I pray also for those who believe in me through the word that they share; I have given them the glory you gave me so they may be as one with us and be perfected into one in us."

At Supper: Luke 22:15–22

Jesus then said to them, "I have earnestly desired to eat this Passover with you before I suffer, for I will not eat of it again until it is fulfilled in the kingdom of God. My body is given for you."

He took bread, blessed it, gave thanks, and broke it and gave it to them, saying, "Do this in memory of me."

Do this in memory of me
Courtesy of the lumoproject.com

In the same way, he took the cup after supper, saying,
"This cup is the new covenant in my blood, which will be poured out for you.
The Son of Man goes as it has been determined, but woe to that man through whom he is betrayed."

Jesus Predicts His Betrayal: Luke 22:21–23; John 13:18–26; Matthew 26:21–25

"I don't speak concerning all of you. I know who I have chosen. But that the Scripture may be fulfilled, 'He who eats bread with me has lifted up his heel against me.' I am telling this now before it happens so that when it happens you may believe that I am he."

Jesus became troubled in spirit and testified, "I tell you truly, one of you is going to betray me."

The disciples looked at one another, perplexed about whom he spoke. One of them, the disciple Jesus loved, was reclining next to him.

Simon Peter beckoned and said, "Ask him which one he means."

The disciple leaned back against Jesus and asked, "Lord, who is it?"

Jesus answered: "The man who has dipped his hand into the bowl is the one who will betray me. The Son of Man is departing just as it is written of him, but woe to that man through whom the Son of Man is betrayed. It would be better for him if he had never been born."

As Jesus was dipping into the bowl with Judas, he said to him quietly, "Be quick about what you are to do."

No sooner had Judas eaten the morsel than he went out into the night.

After singing songs of praise, they walked out to the Mount of Olives.

Peter's Denial Foretold: Matthew 26:31–35; Luke 22:31–37

Jesus said to them, "All of you will be made to stumble, because of me tonight, for it is written, 'I will strike the shepherd and the sheep of the flock will be scattered.' But after I am raised up, I will go before you into Galilee."

Peter answered, "Even if all will be made to stumble because of you, I will never be made to stumble."

Jesus replied, "Simon, Simon, Satan has asked that all of you be sifted as wheat; but I have prayed for you that your faith wouldn't fail and when you have turned back, strengthen your brothers."

But he replied, "Lord, I am ready to go with you to prison and to death."

Jesus said, "I tell you, Peter, before the rooster crows today, you will deny three times that you know me."

Then Jesus asked them, "When I sent you out without purse, bag, or sandals, did you lack for anything?"

"Nothing," they answered.

He said to them, "Now if you have a purse, take it as well as a bag; if you don't have a sword, sell your cloak and buy one. What is written must still be fulfilled in me."

The disciples said, "Lord, here are two swords."

Jesus replied, "That is enough."

The Agony in the Garden: Luke 22:39–46; Matthew 26:38–46

Jesus went out as usual to the Mount of Olives and his disciples followed.

On reaching a place called Gethsemane, he said to them, "My soul is exceedingly sorrowful, even to death. Stay here and watch with me."

He went forward a little, fell down on his face, and prayed, "Father, if it is possible, let this cup pass away from me; nevertheless, not what I desire, but what you desire."

Agony at Gethsemane
Courtesy of Jan van't Hoff collection

Being in anguish, he prayed more earnestly, and his sweat was like drops of blood on the ground. He rose from prayer and went back to the disciples and found them asleep.

He said to them, "Why do you sleep? Rise and pray that you will not fall into temptation."

The Arrest: Matthew 26:47–56; Luke 22:47–54; Mark 14:43–52

As he was speaking, a crowd formed armed with swords and clubs with Judas leading them. He approached Jesus to kiss him, but Jesus asked him, "Judas, are you betraying the Son of Man with a kiss?"

As they stepped forward to seize Jesus, one of those with him drew his sword and cut off the ear of the high priest's servant.

Jesus said, "No more of this; those that draw the sword will die by the sword."

He touched the man's ear and healed him; he said to the crowd, "Have you come out as against a robber with swords and clubs to seize me? I sat daily in the temple teaching, and you didn't arrest me. But all this is happening that the scriptures of the prophets might be fulfilled."

At that, the disciples deserted him and fled; one was only covered with a loincloth, and as they tried to seize him, he left the cloth behind and ran away naked.

Before the Sanhedrin: Matthew 26:57–68

They led him off to Caiaphas, the high priest where the scribes and elders were gathered. Peter followed at a distance and went into the courtyard. He sat around a fire with the guard to see the end. The whole Sanhedrin sought false testimony against Jesus, that they might put him to death, but found none. One example was that Jesus had said, "I am able to destroy the temple of God and rebuild it in three days."

Finally, Caiaphas said, "Have you no answer to the testimony levelled against you?" But Jesus held his peace.

Then the high priest said, "I adjure you by the living God to tell us whether you are the Messiah, the Son of God."

Jesus answered, "It is you who say it; and I tell you after this you will see the Son of Man sitting at the right hand of Power and coming on the clouds of the sky."

At this, the high priest tore his robes and said, "He has spoken blasphemy; why do we need any more witnesses? What do you think?"

They answered, "He is worthy of death."

They mocked him and spit on him and beat him.

Peter's Denial: Matthew 26:69–75; Luke 22:55–62

A servant girl saw Peter sitting in the firelight; she looked intently at him and said, "This man was with him."

But he denied it, saying, "Woman, I don't know him."

A short time later someone else said to him, "You also are one of them."

But Peter answered, "Man, I am not."

A little later some bystanders said to Peter, "You are certainly one of them; your accent is Galilean."

Peter began to curse and swear, saying, "I do not know what you are talking about."

Just then a rooster began to crow, and Peter remembered the prediction Jesus had made. He went outside and wept bitterly.

At daybreak the Sanhedrin took formal action against Jesus to ordered him put to death. They bound him and led him away to be handed over to the procurator, Pilate.

The End of Judas: Matthew 27:3–10

Then Judas, seeing that Jesus had been condemned, began to feel remorse regret for what he had done. He took the thirty pieces of silver back to the leaders and said, "I have sinned in that I betrayed innocent blood."

They said, "What is that to us? You see to it."

Judas threw down the pieces of silver in the sanctuary and departed. He went away and hanged himself. The leaders picked up the money, and since it was not lawful to put it in the treasury since it was the price of blood, they used it to buy the potter's field to be used for burying strangers.

Before Pilate and Herod: Luke 22:66–71; 23:1–25; Matthew 27:11–30; John 18:28–40

Jesus was brought before Pilate, who asked, "Are you the son of God?"

Jesus responded, "You say it, because I am."

Then Pilate announced to the chief priests and the crowd, "I find no basis for a charge against this man."

But they insisted: "He stirs up the people all over Judea by his teaching; he started in Galilee and has come all the way here."

When Pilate heard that, as a Galilean, he was under Herod's jurisdiction. He sent him to Herod, who was in Jerusalem at the time.

Herod was exceedingly glad to see Jesus, hoping that he would perform some miracles for him. He asked Jesus many questions, but Jesus gave no answer to any of the accusations from the chief priests and teachers of the law. Herod and his soldiers humiliated and mocked him, dressed him in luxurious clothing, and sent him back to Pilate.

At this, Pilate said to the whole assembly, "I have examined him in your presence and have found no basis for your charges against him, nor has Herod; nothing worthy of death has been done by him. I will therefore chastise him and release him."

At the feast, the governor was accustomed to release one prisoner whom they desired to the multitude. Pilate offered them a choice between Barabbas, who was in prison for insurrection and murder, and Jesus.

He said, "Which of the two do you want me to release to you?"

The crowd shouted, "Away with this man; release Barabbas to us."

Pilate went back into the praetorium and said to Jesus, "So then are you the king of the Jews?"

Jesus answered, "For this reason, I was born. The reason I came into the world is to testify to the truth; everyone who is of the truth listens to my voice."

"Truth," Pilate said, "What does that mean?"

Pilate then had Jesus flogged, and the soldiers twisted thorns into a crown and put it on his head. They dressed him in a garment of royal purple, saying, "Hail, King of the Jews."

Pilate then brought Jesus out in front of the crowd and said, "Look at the man!"

As soon as the crowd saw him, the temple guard stirred them up, shouting, "Crucify him, crucify him!"

Pilate realized the anger of the crowd was boiling over. He said, "Shall I crucify your king?"

The chief priests replied, "We have no king but Caesar!"

When Pilate saw he was getting nowhere, he took water and washed his hands in front of the crowd. He said, "I am innocent of this man's blood; it is your responsibility."

All the people answered, "His blood is on us and on our children."

In the end, Pilate handed Jesus over to be crucified.

The Crucifixion: Luke 23:26–43; Matthew 27:32–44; John 19:17–24

The soldiers removed the purple robe and put his own clothes back on him and led him out to crucify him. As they led him out, they grabbed one Simon of Cyrene, coming in from the country, and laid on him the cross to carry after Jesus. Pilate had an inscription placed on the cross, which read "Jesus of Nazareth, King of the Jews."

The chief priests said to Pilate, "Don't write 'The King of the Jews,' but 'He said I am King of the Jews.'"

Pilate answered, "What I have written, I have written."

A great multitude followed, including women who mourned and lamented him.

He turned and said, "Daughters of Jerusalem, don't weep for me, but for yourselves and your children; the time will come when they will say, 'Blessed are the barren, the women that never bore, and the breasts that never nursed.'"

On arriving at a place called Golgotha (Skull Place), they tried giving him some wine drugged with myrrh, but he would not take it. Then they crucified him along with two criminals, one on each side of him.

Jesus said, "Father, forgive them, for they don't know what they are doing."

They divided up his clothes between them, but with the tunic, which was woven from top to bottom, they cast lots.

One of the criminals who hung there, hurled insults at him and said, "If you are the Messiah, save yourself and us."

The other criminal rebuked him and said, "Don't you even fear God, seeing as we are under the same condemnation? We are receiving what our deeds deserve, but this man has done nothing wrong." Then he said to Jesus, "Lord, remember me when you come into your kingdom."

Jesus said, "Assuredly I tell you; today you will be with me in Paradise."

Those who passed by made such comments as, "He saved others, but he can't save himself"; "If he's the king of Israel, let him come down from the cross and we will believe in him"; and "He said he is the Son of God. Let God rescue him now if he wants him."

The Death of Jesus: Luke 23:44–46; Matthew 27:45–51; John 19:25–36

Near the cross stood his mother, his mother's sister Mary, the wife of Cleopas, and Mary Magdalene. Seeing his mother there with the disciple whom he loved, he said, "Woman, look at your son." And to the disciple: "Look to your mother."

From then on, she became a member of the disciple's family.

From noon onward darkness descended over the land, and near midafternoon, Jesus said, "My God, my God, why have you forsaken me?"

Then, knowing that everything had now been finished and scripture would be fulfilled, he said, "I am thirsty."

They soaked a sponge in wine vinegar and put it to his lips on the end of a stalk of the hyssop plant.

When he received the drink, Jesus said, "It is finished." He bowed his head and gave up his spirit.

Suddenly, the curtain of the sanctuary was torn from top to bottom, the earth quaked, and boulders split. The centurion and his men who were keeping watch were terrified at all that was happening and said, "Certainly this was a righteous man."

Death of Jesus
Courtesy of Jan van't Hoff collection

The Burial: Luke 23:50–56; John, 19:31–42; Matthew, 27:57–61

Seeing as the next day was the Sabbath, the Jewish leaders did not want the bodies left on the crosses. One of them, Joseph of Arimathea, a distinguished member of the Sanhedrin who had not consented to their counsel and deed, boldly went to Pilate and asked for Jesus's body. The soldiers came and broke the legs of the two criminals, but when they came to Jesus, they found him already dead, so they didn't break his legs. But one pierced his side with a lance, bringing a sudden flow of blood and water. Even this act fulfilled the scriptures: "Not one of his bones will be broken," as well as "They will look on him who they have pierced." Learning that he was already dead, Pilate released the body to Joseph.

Accompanied by Nicodemus, the one who had secretly met Jesus earlier, they came and took the body away, wrapped it in strips of linen with a mixture of myrrh and aloes, and laid it in a new tomb, which had been cut out of rock. Finally, they rolled a stone across the entrance.

The chief priests went to Pilate and said, "We remember that this deceiver had said he would rise again after three days. Command, therefore, that the tomb be made secure until the third day, lest his disciples come at night and steal him away and tell the people, 'He is risen from the dead.'" Pilate said," You have your own guard; go and secure the tomb as best you can."

They put a guard on the tomb and a seal on the entrance.

9

Triumph

Why are you looking for the living among the dead
Courtesy of the lumo project.com

The Resurrection

The Tale of the Guards

Jesus Appears to Mary Magdalene

On the Road to Emmaus

Jesus Appears to His Disciples

Yeshua returns to Yahweh

The Empty Tomb: Luke 24:1–12

Early on the first day of the week, Mary Magdalene and Mary, the mother of James and Salome, went to the tomb, bringing the perfume and spices they had prepared. They had been concerned about the stone across the entrance, but when they got there, they found it had already been rolled back. On entering the tomb, they saw two young men dressed in clothes that gleamed like lightning sitting there. Becoming terrified, they bowed their faces down to the earth.

"Don't be frightened," one said. "Why are you looking for the living among the dead? Jesus is not here; he has risen."

They departed quickly from the tomb with fear and great joy and ran to bring his disciples word.

The disciples thought these words were nonsense.

Joanna and the others with them confirmed the story, but they didn't believe them.

The Tale of the Guards: Matthew 28:11–15

As the women were returning, some of the guards came into the city and told the chief priests all the things that had happened. The chief priests, in turn, assembled with the elders and took counsel; they gave a large amount of silver to the soldiers and said, "Tell them his disciples came by night and stole him away while we slept. We will talk to the governor."

They took the money and did as they were told. This saying was spread abroad among the Jews and continues until this day.

Jesus Appears to Mary Magdalene: John 20:11–18

Peter got up and went to the tomb. Stooping and looking in, he saw the strips of linen lying there and went away, wondering what had happened.

Mary Magdalene was distraught and went back to the tomb in tears. As she stood there, she turned around and saw a man standing there, not knowing it was Jesus who said to her, "Woman, why are you weeping? Who are you are looking for?"

She said to him, "Sir, they have taken my Lord away; if you are the one who has carried him off, tell me where you have laid him, and I will go and take him away."

Jesus said to her, "Mary!"

She turned toward him and cried out in Aramaic, "*Rabboni*!"

Jesus said to her, "Don't touch me as I haven't yet ascended to my Father; go to my brothers and tell them, 'I am ascending to my Father and your Father, to my God and your God.'"

She came to the disciples with the news, "I have seen the Lord." And she told them all the things he had spoken to her.

On the Road to Emmaus: Luke 24:13–35

On that same day, two of them were going to a village named Emmaus, about seven miles from Jerusalem. As they walked, they talked with each other about all of these things that had happened. While they talked and questioned together, it happened that Jesus himself came near and went with them. But their eyes were kept from recognizing him.

He asked them, "What are you talking about as you walk, and are sad?"

One of them, Cleopas, said, "Are you the only stranger in Jerusalem who doesn't know the things that have happened there in these days."

Jesus said, "What things?"

They said to him, "The things concerning Jesus, the Nazarene, who was a prophet, mighty in deed and in word before God and all the people; and how the chief priests and our rulers delivered him up to be condemned to death and crucified him. We were hoping that it was he who would redeem Israel. Besides all this, it is now the third day since these things happened, and certain women of our company went to the tomb and didn't find his body. They said they had seen a vision of angels who said he is alive. He said to them, 'Foolish men and slow of heart to believe in all that the prophets have spoken, didn't the Messiah have to suffer these things to enter into his glory?' Then he explained all the things, right back from Moses, that had been said concerning him.

"They drew near to the village where they were going, and Jesus made as if to go on, but they urged him to stay, as it was getting late. He went in to stay with them. When he sat at table, he took bread, gave thanks, broke it, and gave it to them. Their eyes were opened.

He then disappeared from their sight.

They got up and returned at once to Jerusalem, where they found the disciples assembled together, and said to them, "It is true, the Lord has risen and has appeared to Simon."

Jesus Appears to his Disciples: Luke 24:36–49

While they were still talking about this, Jesus himself appeared among them and said, "Peace be with you."

They were quite startled, thinking they were seeing a ghost.

He said to them, "Why are you troubled, and why do doubts arise in your hearts? Look at my hands and feet; it is really me! Thomas, come and touch me! A spirit doesn't have flesh and bones as you see I do. Is there anything to eat here?"

They gave him a piece of broiled fish, which he ate in front of them. He said, "This is why I told you while I was still with you that all things that have been written about me in the law of Moses, the prophets, and the psalms must be fulfilled."

He opened their minds so they could understand the scriptures and said, "The Messiah will suffer and rise from the dead on the third day, and repentance for the remittance of sins will be preached in his name to all nations, beginning at Jerusalem. You are witnesses of these things. I am going to send what my Father has promised, but stay in the city until you have been clothed in power from on high. Know that I am with you always until the end of the world!"

Jeshua returns to Jahweh
Courtesy Jan van't Hoff collection

Yeshua Returns to Yahweh: Luke 24:50–53

Then he led them out to the vicinity of Bethany; he lifted up his eyes and blessed them. While he was blessing them, he withdrew from them and was carried up into heaven. Yeshua was returning to Yahweh. The disciples worshipped him and returned to Jerusalem with great joy to await the arrival of the Holy Spirit.

EPILOGUE

Poem by Leo
Soulétude

The sun in silent solace sinks
Beneath the azure sea.
It's then I know beyond all doubt
You are Your Majesty!
I see your face in every cloud;
You see me from the stars,
Each one of us in silent talk
Whispers beyond Mars.

The mountain ranges beckon me
As do the tranquil lakes.
In sunshine, sleet, and even snow
I'm yet to find mistakes.
In awesome grandeur of a canyon,
Aware am I of you.
Your closeness all of me surrounds
And I am born anew.
No need have I to sit inside
Some dim-lit church or hall
And babble like the pagans do;
I haven't got the gall.

Cathedral is, for me, out here
From desert sands to sea;
You've placed each minute bit of dust
As it was meant to be.
And then there are of course the birds
And all your creatures true.
In joyful harmony they cry;
Each chorus is for you.
I can't construct a prayer that sweet—
In silence I remain.
You know my thoughts in any case;
I'll muse on the refrain.
Incredible it is to me
How vast this land became.
It's like it's just for thee and me—
Yet others feel the same.
Black starlit skies hold me in awe.
I'm almost next to nothing.
And then a supernova glows
Light years and amazing
Galaxies on galaxies beyond;
There must be life out there!
Yet man is really not much more
Beyond the stratosphere.
Then next, a softly moonlit bay
Enraptures me complete.
I am imbued with love again,
So totally replete.

The never-ending scenes unfold
With every passing day.
Were I but able to record
Each one before I lay.
Yet onward, upward, outward too
The dreamer journeys on,
And every incident is new,
Each footstep is a song.
The dreaming stories well portray
In legend, myth, and lore,
Formation of each little piece
Of such a vast jigsaw.
And this is just a small account
In time and place and space,
As here I try to comprehend
Such magnitude and grace.
In solitude some silent night
When face to face I'll be,
Acknowledging in all of this
You are Your Majesty!

Ingram Content Group UK Ltd.
Milton Keynes UK
UKHW050119080723
424737UK00003BA/29

9 781973 699989